In This Book

QuickStart Guide

Your keys to understanding the island – we help you decide what to do and how to do it

Need to Know
Tips for a smooth trip

Regions
What's where

Explore Bali

The best things to see and do, area by area

Top Experiences
Make the most of your visit

Local Life
The insider's island

The Best of Bali

The island's highlights in handy lists to help you plan

Best Walks
See the region on foot

Bali's Best...
The best experiences

Survival Guide

Tips and tricks for a seamless, hassle-free island experience

Getting Around
Travel like a local

Essential Information
Including where to stay

Our selection of the regions's best places to eat, drink and experience:

◉ **Experiences**

❌ **Eating**

🅞 **Drinking**

✪ **Entertainment**

🅐 **Shopping**

These symbols give you the vital information for each listing:

☎ Telephone Numbers	👶 Family-Friendly
⊘ Opening Hours	🐾 Pet-Friendly
🅟 Parking	🚌 Bus
🚭 Nonsmoking	⛴ Ferry
@ Internet Access	Ⓜ Metro
🛜 Wi-Fi Access	Ⓢ Subway
🥗 Vegetarian Selection	🚋 Tram
📖 English-Languag Menu	🚆 Train

Find each listing quickly on maps for each region:

Bar Hemingway

16 🅞 Map p233, B2

Legend has it that Hemi self, wielding a machine iberate this timber-pan ered bar during showpiece is a en by Papa ar town. Dress s.com; Hôtel Rit ⊘6.30pm-2a

Lonely Planet's Bali

Lonely Planet Pocket Guides are designed to get you straight to the heart of the region.

Inside you'll find all the must-see sights, plus tips to make your visit to each one really memorable. We've split the city into easy-to-navigate neighbourhoods and provided clear maps so you'll find your way around with ease. Our expert authors have searched out the best of the city: walks, food, nightlife and shopping, to name a few. Because you want to explore, our 'Local Life' pages will take you to some of the most exciting areas to experience the real Bali.

And of course you'll find all the practical tips you need for a smooth trip: itineraries for short visits, how to get around, and how much to tip the guy who serves you a drink at the end of a long day's exploration.

It's your guarantee of a really great experience.

Our Promise

You can trust our travel information because Lonely Planet authors visit the places we write about, each and every edition. We never accept freebies for positive coverage, so you can rely on us to tell it like it is.

The Best of Bali 129

Bali's Best Walks

Bali's Best ...

Survival Guide 147

QuickStart Guide

Welcome to Bali

Bali's rich culture plays out at all levels of life, from the exquisite flower-petal offerings placed everywhere to the processions of joyfully garbed locals to the traditional music and dance. Add in great beaches, world-class surfing, superb dining, stunning sunsets, beautiful walks and fabulous shopping, and Bali is simply unbeatable.

Gamelan ensemble (p97), Penestanan
MANFRED GOTTSCHALK/GETTY IMAGES ©

Bali
Top Experiences

Feeling Spiritual at Pura Luhur Batukau (p58)

A multitiered, Kyoto-esque temple rises out of the mists cloaking the side of one of Bali's main volcanoes. You've reached Pura Luhur Batukau, where you can feel the island's sacred magic.

JOHN SEATON CALLAHAN/GETTY IMAGES ©

Hanging Out at Ulu Watu's Beaches (p68)

Bali's own version of pearls, the string of beaches towards Ulu Watu has some of the island's best sand shimmering in the sunlight. Enjoy the adventure of reaching these often-isolated locations.

MARTIN PUDDY/GETTY IMAGES ©

Touring Ubud's Rice Fields (p100)

Ribbons of green sinuously curving around hillsides crested by coconut palms and emerald patchworks blanketing the land: these are some of the vistas you'll savour as you walk Ubud's rice fields.

Nusa Lembongan (p90)

Lazing on a beach, riding a wave, meeting a parrotfish while snorkelling, coming face to face with a sunfish while diving in deep clear waters: these moments define Nusa Lembongan.

SCUBAZOO/GETTY IMAGES ©

Gili Trawangan (p126)

An all-day, all-night party, that's Gili T – take a fast boat over from Bali to whoop it up. Divers can also find briny joy and snorkellers will discover under-water beauty right off the beach.

RANDI ANG/GETTY IMAGES ©

Bali
Local Life

Insider tips to help you find the real island

After checking out Bali's top experiences, find out what makes this magnificent island tick. Discover the beauty of sunsets from the beaches and savour the culture and purely Balinese lifestyle in Ubud.

Beach Walk: Batubelig to Echo Beach (p48)

▶ Deserted beaches
▶ Isolated temples

At its busiest, Kuta Beach can feel like you've stumbled into a flash mob. The same goes for Legian and even Seminyak's beaches. But head north along this seemingly limitless arc of sand from Batubelig Beach and you'll leave Bali's crowds behind, see seldom-visited temples and have a grand adventure. The steady pace of development means that glitzy days for this stretch of sand are just around the corner, so go now while you can still say it's a naturally beautiful domain.

A Perfect Ubud Day (p102)

▶ Alluring shopping
▶ A cleansed body

If one Ubud is all about Balinese creativity and culture, another Ubud is much more inwardly focused. On this stroll you can get your body purged of poisons, fill it with healthy nourishment, adorn it with beauty and, bringing things full circle, feel the inspiration of Balinese dance. In fact, it is a good thing that Ubud is blessed with so many fine cafes, as otherwise you might find yourself so caught up in the pleasures of wandering its lanes that you'd forget to enjoy a break.

Kuta Beach (p26)

Legong dancer (p97)

Other great ways to experience Bali like a local:

Sunset drinks on the Legian Beach sand (p31)

Seminyak sunsets at a beach bar (p42)

Seminyak shopping (p44)

Kerobokan's favourite warung (p53)

Canggu's cafes (p56)

Benoa's places of worship (p80)

Sanur's kites (p89)

Ubud's library (p109)

Gay Seminyak (p39)

Gianyar's Tasty Night Market (p124)

Bali
Day Planner

Day One

Spend your first day in Bali's tourism heart. Begin by learning to surf Kuta Beach's reliable waves at **Pro Surf School** (p27). Or learn yoga at Kerobokan's **Desa Seni** (p52). Of course you could let others do the work at the famous Seminyak spas **Prana** (p38) and **Jari Menari** (p38). No matter what, enjoy breakfast at **Biku** (p39) or Canggu's **Monsieur Spoon** (p56).

With the sun high overhead, hit **Kuta Beach** (p26) or **Double Six Beach** (p26). Or take shelter from the rays overhead with a little shopping in Seminyak at retail-icious spots like **Lily Jean** (p45) and **Bathe** (p42) on Jl Petitenget. For lunch go local at **Warung Sulawesi** (p53) or **Warung Eny** (p53).

Don't miss sunset drinks in the west. Buy a beer from vendors at **Legian Beach** (p26) or go more upscale at trendy **Potato Head** (p41) or at one of the Seminyak's **beach shacks** (p37). Dinner calls for something great in Kerobokan: classy **Sardine** (p56) or **Sarong** (p56), or the simplicity of **Warung Sobat** (p55). Close out the night at Kuta's party that never ends starting at **Sky Garden Lounge** (p32).

Day Two

This day puts you deep into Bali's cultural soul on the island's volcanic slopes. Go early before anyone else to **Pura Luhur Batukau** (p59), where you'll find a sacred temple on the slopes of its namesake volcano. Afterwards, stop to enjoy the rice fields of **Jatiluwih** (p59) before driving east up and down the ridges of lush foothills to Ubud.

After a morning of Balinese culture, have a healthy lunch at **Bali Buda** (p110) or **Warung Soba** (p103), or try the fabulous porky fare at **Warung Ibu Oka** (p110). After, seek serenity at **Yoga Barn** (p108) or **Bali Botanica Day Spa** (p108). Do it yourself with a walk through **Ubud's rice fields** (p100).

One Bali experience not to be missed is a traditional dance show in Ubud. Choose your **dance performance** (p114) and watch the dancers go through their precise motions to the cacophony of the gamelan. After, fine dinner choices include **Locavore** (p113) or one of many good places on Jl Dewi Sita. Bedtime is early in the cool mountain air; enjoy the symphony of insects as you shut your eyes.

Short on time?

We've arranged Bali's must-sees into these day-by-day itineraries to make sure you see the very best of the island in the time you have available.

Day Three

Using Sanur as your hub, start in Denpasar at the markets, **Pasar Badung** (p96) and **Pasar Kumbasari** (p96), when selections are the freshest. Afterwards lay low for a bit on **Sanur Beach** (p86), maybe doing a bit of swimming in the mellow waters.

Have lunch at one of the places along the coast road such as **Merta Sari** (p124) and then swing up to the rice fields and lush green hills along the **Sidemen Road** (p121). See if you can catch a glimpse of Bali's most important volcano, the often-cloud-shrouded Gunung Agung. Head south to **Semarapura** (p121) and the historically important **Taman Kertha Gosa** (p125).

Back in Sanur, get in some spa time at **Jamu Traditional Spa** (p85), then hit Jl Tamblingan for some shopping: Bali-designed goods at **A-Krea** (p89) and a recommended read at **Ganesha Bookshop** (p89). Wiggle your toes in the sand for dinner at **Warung Pantai Indah** (p88) or go more upscale at **Minami** (p88) or **Three Monkeys Cafe** (p89).

Day Four

Spend your day south of the airport in the many-splendoured but still compact Bukit Peninsula. In the morning, don't miss Jimbaran's **Fish Market** (p63), or engage hands-on with your food at the renowned **Bumbu Bali Cooking School** (p79). After, get soaked in the family fun of water sports at **Benoa Marine Recreation** (p80) or surf legendary breaks such as **Ulu Watu** (p72).

Behold beautiful Balinese art in the shady **Pasifika Museum** (p79) or follow the smart set to one of the beach coves such as **Balangan** (p72), **Bingin** (p73) or **Padang Padang** (p72). Each offers cafes on the sand and fine waters for a plunge.

As the sun creates its ever-changing daily show in the west, wander through the fragrant smoke of the three main areas of Jimbaran's **seafood warungs** (p65) to find your spot for dinner or at least a sunset drink. Alternatively, head to **Pura Luhur Ulu Watu** (p71) for sunset and the **dance performance** (p75) that follows. For the best Balinese meal you'll have, consider dinner at **Bumbu Bali** (p81).

Need to Know

For more information, see Survival Guide (p147)

Currency
Rupiah (Rp)

Language
Bahasa Indonesia and Balinese

Visas
Usually 30 days, purchased on arrival.

Money
ATMs in south Bali, Ubud and tourist areas. Credit cards accepted at midrange and top-end hotels and restaurants.

Mobile Phones
Local SIM cards work with any unlocked GSM phone.

Time
WIT (Central Indonesian Standard Time; GMT/UTC plus eight hours)

Plugs & Adaptors
Plugs have two round pins like Europe; electrical current is 220V. Australian and North American visitors will require plug adaptors; most electronic devices can handle 110V or 220V.

Tipping
10% for service workers is greatly appreciated.

① Before You Go

Your Daily Budget

Budget less than US$80

▶ Room in guesthouse/homestay less than US$50

▶ Cheap food and drink, even at fairly nice places

▶ Can survive on US$25 per day

Midrange US$80 to US$220

▶ Room in midrange hotel US$50 to US$150

▶ Can eat and drink virtually anywhere

▶ Can enjoy spa treatments and other luxuries

Top end more than US$220

▶ Room in top-end hotel/resort more than US$150

▶ Major expenses will be lavish spas

▶ Luxury boutiques await

Useful Websites

▶ **Bali Advertiser** (www.baliadvertiser.biz) Local news and a variety of columnists with useful information.

▶ **Bali Discovery** (www.balidiscovery.com) Has an essential and first-rate Bali news section and a wealth of other island information.

▶ **Lonely Planet** (www.lonelyplanet.com/indonesia/bali) Destination information, hotel bookings, traveller forum and more.

Advance Planning

Three months before Book rooms during high season.

One month before Book rooms during shoulder season.

One week before Book top restaurants and spas during high season.

Arriving in Bali

From Bali's airport, your main choices of transport are either pre-arranged rides through your hotel or villa or prepaid taxis. The former cost US$10 to US$50, the latter vary by destination.

✈ From Ngurah Rai Airport

Destination	Best Transport
Kuta & Legian	Taxi
Seminyak	Taxi
Kerobokan	Taxi
Sanur	Taxi
Ubud	Taxi

✈ At the Airport

Ngurah Rai Airport Bali's airport (DPS; listed as Denpasar or Bali on travel websites) has a disappointing and poorly designed new terminal. The arrivals area has ATMs and moneychangers. Avoid the porters. What's called 'duty free' has inflated prices and offers no bargains on Bali's high wine and spirits prices. Accommodation services may book you into inconvenient locations.

Getting Around

Taxis are the most common means of transport. However, no matter what your mode, everyone is affected by the same awful traffic in south Bali and Ubud.

🚗 Taxi

Cheap, widely available and easy to hail in south Bali. Always insist on the meter, although most will automatically use it in the daytime. Bluebird Taxis are the most reliable. In Ubud, freelance drivers charge US$2 to US$5 for rides around town.

🚗 Car & Driver

Very common for longer trips and all-day touring. Can be arranged through your hotel; they cost US$50 to US$60 per day.

Walking

The best way to get around the Kuta–Legian–Seminyak, Nusa Dua–Tanjung Benoa and Sanur areas (often on pleasant beachfront walkways), as well as Ubud.

🚗 Car

Car rentals are often arranged from streetside vendors. Cheap and adventurous, but you are at the mercy of Bali's traffic and it's very easy to get lost.

Motorbike

Cheap and easily arranged, and you can weave around traffic if you are a daredevil; can be very dangerous.

🚌 Tourist Bus

Cheap air-con buses operated by Perama Tours, among others, on a limited network that covers Kuta–Sanur–Ubud–Padangbai.

Bali
Regions

Pura Luhur Batukau

Denpasar (p92)
Bali's sprawling, chaotic capital is the island's population hub. Look for museums and monuments plus vibrant shopping and eating.

Kerobokan & Canggu (p46)
Villas and surfer guesthouses mingle with rice fields and fine dining. Beaches range from lonely to trendy; the waves are bigger than further south.

Seminyak (p34)
Streets lined with designer boutiques and shops of every sort; oodles of good restaurants, and the beach is never far away.

Kuta & Legian (p22)
Bali's chaotic heart of mass tourism has squawking vendors and sweaty clubs all jammed in tight against a legendary beach.

Ulu Watu & Around (p66)
Pocket-sized white-sand beaches sit in coves below cliffs. Bamboo cafes cater to surfers and their fans.

Ulu Watu's Beaches

⊙ Top Experiences
Hanging out at Ulu Watu's beaches

Jimbaran (p60)
A low-key bay and beach; the action is at the famous fish market and dozens of beachside grilled-seafood joints.

Ubud's Rice Fields

Ubud (p98)
Bali's cultural heart is an alluring mix of creative boutiques, spas and cultural performances.

👁 **Top Experiences**

Touring Ubud's rice fields

Nusa Lembongan

Sanur (p82)
Combines Balinese style with a thriving expat community. The quiet beach is perfect for families too mature for Kuta.

East Bali (p118)
In the shadow of Gunung Agung, Bali's most important volcano, enjoy black-sand beaches, historic sights and impossibly green vistas.

Nusa Dua & Tanjung Benoa (p76)
Fronted by a reef-protected beach, Nusa Dua is a gated top-end resort world, while Tanjung Benoa caters to midrange groups.

Worth a Trip
👁 **Top Experiences**

Pura Luhur Batukau

Nusa Lembongan

Gili Trawangan

Explore
Bali

Traditional Balinese dancers, Pura Dalem Ubud (p114)
RUDI VAN STARREX/GETTY IMAGES ©

Explore

Kuta & Legian

Teeming, mad, crazy, wild, loud. Those are a few words that describe Kuta and Legian, the original tourist centre of Bali and the place that everyone either loves to hate or loves to love. Kuta's the original, with its *gangs* (narrow alleys), hawkers, tawdry bars, cheap hotels and all-night clubs. Legian is pretty much the same, albeit for a slightly older crowd.

The Region in a Day

☀ Start your day taking advantage of Bali's ever-reliable waves by learning to surf at one of the good schools such as **Pro Surf School** (p27). After a couple of hours in the water, join late-risers and all-night clubbers for an early lunch. The north end of Legian offers good choices: try either **Warung Asia** (p28) or **Warung Murah** (p29).

☀ In the afternoon, if time by the hotel pool doesn't divert you, head out for some serious beach action at **Kuta Beach** (p26), **Legian Beach** (p26) or **Double Six Beach** (p26). Or head indoors for some rejuvenating spa action at **Jamu Traditional Spa** (p27) or **Putri Bali** (p27). Don't miss sunset drinks from vendors on the mellow stretch of **Legian Beach** (p31).

☾ Enjoy creative surfer fare in the hub of the action at **Stakz Bar & Grill** (p30) or go for Asian fusion at **Fat Chow** (p29). Now prepare for the all-night party march, the number-one reason people flock to Kuta. Check the happy hour schedule and follow the crowds from one club to the next. Make **Sky Garden Lounge** (p32) your hub, with forays to surrounding venues.

💙 **Best of Bali**

Surf Breaks
Kuta Beach (p26)

Double Six Beach (p26)

Surf Schools
Pro Surf School (p27)

Rip Curl School of Surf (p28)

Beaches
Kuta Beach (p26)

Nightlife
Sky Garden Lounge (p32)

Pampering
Jamu Traditional Spa (p27)

Shopping
Surfer Girl (p33)

Bali For Kids
Rip Curl School of Surf (p28)

Waterbom Park (p26)

❶ Getting There & Around

🚗 **Taxi** Taxis from the airport, which is just south of Kuta, will cost 40,000Rp to 60,000Rp.

Walk You can easily walk all of Kuta and Legian, the beach is always the most pleasant; Jl Legian is filled with aggressive vendors.

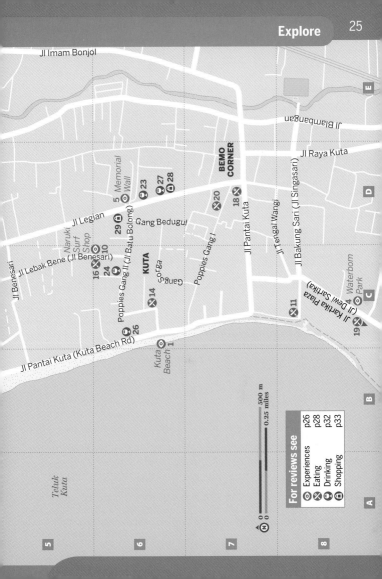

Jl Imam Bonjol

Jl Blambangan

Jl Raya Kuta

BEMO CORNER

5 Memorial Wall

● 23

● 27 ● 28

Jl Legian

29 ●

Gang Bedugul

● 20

18 ●

Naruki Surf Shop

● 10

Jl Lebak Bene (Jl Benesari)

16 ● 24

Jl Benesari

Poppies Gang II (Jl Batu Bolong)

KUTA

Sorga Gang

Poppies Gang I

Jl Pantai Kuta

Jl Tengal Wangi

Jl Bakung Sari (Jl Singasari)

Jl Kartika Plaza (Jl Dewi Sartika)

Waterbom Park

● 11

19 ▲

● 14

26 ●

Jl Pantai Kuta (Kuta Beach Rd)

Kuta Beach ● 1

Teluk Kuta

500 m
0.25 miles

For reviews see	
◉ Experiences	p26
◉⊗ Eating	p28
◉ Drinking	p32
◉ Shopping	p33

Experiences

Kuta Beach
BEACH

1 Map p24, C6

Tourism in Bali began here and is there any question why? Surf that started far out in the Indian Ocean crashes to shore in long symmetrical breaks. Low-key hawkers will sell you soft drinks and beer, snacks and other treats, and you can rent surfboards, lounge chairs and umbrellas (negotiable at 10,000Rp to 20,000Rp) or just crash on the sand.

Legian Beach
BEACH

2 Map p24, B3

An extension of Kuta Beach to the south, Legian Beach is quieter thanks to the lack of a raucous road next to the sand and fewer people. The section in front of the Sari Beach Hotel is far from any road, is backed by shady trees, is never crowded, has somnolent vendors and isn't crossed by a stream with dubious water. You'll even hear something rarely heard in Kuta: the surf.

Double Six Beach
BEACH

3 Map p24, A1

Very popular, this beach is the northern continuation of Legian Beach. It's alive with pick-up games of football and volleyball all day long and has a perpetual buzz. There are scores of popular beach bars here. One off-note is the stream that crosses the beach, which is a source of unsavoury smells and dubious water.

Top Tip

What's Double Six?

One of Southeast Asia's most famous clubs, Double Six Club, was *the* go-to party choice on Bali for years. But the island's phenomenal growth caught up with it in 2011 and its valuable beachfront real estate now hosts the ultra-hip Double-Six beachfront resort. The namesake beach still has a row of right-on-the-sand bars at the north end.

Waterbom Park
AMUSEMENT PARK

4 Map p24, C8

This watery amusement park covers 3.5 hectares of landscaped tropical gardens. It has assorted water slides, swimming pools and play areas, a supervised park for children under five years old, and a 'lazy river' ride. Other indulgences include the 'pleasure pool', a food court and bar, and a spa. (0361-755676; www.waterbom-bali. com; Jl Kartika Plaza; adult/child US$33/21; 9am-6pm)

Memorial Wall
MONUMENT

5 Map p24, D6

Reflecting the international scope of the 2002 bombings is this memorial wall, where people from many countries pay their respects. Listing the names of the 202 known victims, including 88 Australians and 35 Indonesians, it is starting to look just a touch faded. Across the street, a parking lot

PAUL KENNEDY/GETTY IMAGES ©

Kuta Beach

(with the appalling name 'Ground Zero Legian') is all that is left of the **Sari Club site**. (Jl Legian; ⊘24hr)

Jamu
Traditional Spa   SPA

6 ◎ Map p24, B4

In serene surrounds at a resort hotel, you can enjoy indoor massage rooms that open onto a pretty garden courtyard. If you've ever wanted to be part of a fruit cocktail, here's your chance – treatments involve tropical nuts, coconuts, papayas and more, often in fragrant baths. (☑0361-75250 ext 165; www.jamutraditionalspa.com; Jl Pantai Kuta, Alam Kul Kul; massages from 600,000Rp; ⊘9am-7pm)

Putri Bali   SPA

7 ◎ Map p24, B1

The cream bath here has set the hearts of many spa-ophiles aflutter with delight. This lovely spa has very competitive prices and service that is much more professional than the scads of streetside hawkers. (☑0361-736852; Jl Raya Seminyak 13; massages from 60,000Rp; ⊘9am-9pm)

Pro Surf School   SURFING

8 ◎ Map p24, B4

Right along Kuta Beach, this well-regarded school has been getting beginners standing for years. It offers all levels of lessons. (www.prosurfschool. com; Jl Pantai Kuta; lessons from €45)

NATALIE GRONO/GETTY IMAGES ©

Legian local

Rip Curl School of Surf

SURFING

9 👁 Map p24, A1

Usually, universities sell shirts with their logos; here it's the other way round: the beachwear company sponsors a school. Lessons at all levels are given across the south; there are special courses for kids. They have a location for wakeboarding and kite-surfing in Sanur. (📞0361-735858; www.ripcurlschoolofsurf.com; Jl Arjuna; lessons from 650,000Rp)

Naruki Surf Shop

SURFING

10 👁 Map p24, C6

One of dozens of surf shops lining the lanes of Kuta, the guys here will rent you a board, fix your ding, offer advice or give you lessons. (📞0361-765772; Jl Lebak Bene; ⏱10am-8pm)

Eating

Ajeg Warung

INDONESIAN **$**

11 🍴 Map p24, C8

This simple stall with shady tables is right on Kuta Beach. It dishes up some of the freshest local fare you'll find. Tops is a bowl of spicy *garang asem*, a tamarind-based soup with chicken or pork and many traditional seasonings. Enter the beach where Jl Pantai Kuta turns north and walk south 100m along the beach path. (📞0822 3777 6766; Kuta Beach; meals from 15,000Rp; ⏱8am-8pm)

Warung Asia

ASIAN **$**

12 🍴 Map p24, B1

This very popular cafe serving Asian fare has a great new location on a large leafy courtyard. The food and coffee drinks are as good as ever and now you can enjoy fresh gelato and more. (📞0361-742 0202; Jl Werkudara; meals from 35,000Rp; ⏱8am-10pm; 📶)

Warung Murah INDONESIAN $

13 🍴 Map p24, B1

Lunch goes swimmingly at this authentic warung specialising in seafood. An array of grilled fish awaits; if you prefer fowl over fin, the *satay ayam* is succulent *and* a bargain. Hugely popular at lunch; try to arrive right before noon. (Jl Arjuna; meals from 30,000Rp; ⏱9am-5pm)

Fat Chow ASIAN $$

14 🍴 Map p24, C6

A stylish, modern take on the traditional open-fronted cafe, Fat Chow serves up Chinese and Asian-accented fare at long picnic tables, small tables and loungers. The food is creative with lots of sharing-friendly options. Among the favourites: crunchy Asian salad, pork buns, Tokyo prawns and the Oriental burger. (☎0361-753516; www.fatchowbali.com; Poppies Gang II; mains from 45,000Rp; ⏱10am-10pm)

Take JAPANESE $$

15 🍴 Map p24, D4

Flee Bali for a relaxed version of Tokyo just by ducking under the traditional fabric shield over the doorway at this ever-expanding restaurant. Hyper-fresh sushi, sashimi and more are prepared under the fanatical eyes of a team of chefs behind a long counter. The chef is a stalwart at the Jimbaran fish market in the early

Understand
The Bali Bombings

On Saturday 12 October 2002, two bombs exploded on Kuta's bustling Jl Legian. The first blew out the front of Paddy's Bar. A few seconds later, a far more powerful bomb obliterated the Sari Club. The number of dead, including those unaccounted for, exceeded 200, although the exact number will probably never be known. Many injured Balinese made their way back to their villages, where, for lack of decent medical treatment, they died.

Indonesian authorities eventually laid the blame for the blasts on Jemaah Islamiyah, an Islamic terrorist group that was also behind bombings that killed 20 on Bali in 2005. Dozens were arrested and many were sentenced to jail, including three who received the death penalty (carried out in 2008). But most received relatively light terms, including Abu Bakar Bashir, a radical cleric who many thought was behind the explosions. Umar Patek, who was accused of mixing the explosives used in the bombs, was sentenced to 20 years in jail in 2012.

Although there have been no terrorist attacks on Bali since 2005, concern that it could still be a target remains.

hours. (📞0361-759745; Jl Patih Jelantik; meals 70,000-300,000Rp; ⏱11am-11pm)

Stakz Bar & Grill
INTERNATIONAL $$

16 🍴 Map p24, C6

The notorious nature of the clientele ('bad boy' Australian footballer Todd Carney, noted former prisoner Schapelle Corby) at this very popular Kuta cafe overshadows the excellent food. Top-notch organic fare includes excellent burgers, salads, sandwiches and much more. Lounge on a sofa with a drink and figure out how to get *your* name in the press. (📞0361-762129; www.stakzbarandgrill.com; Jl Benesari; mains 40,000-80,000Rp; ⏱8am-11pm)

Mozarella
ITALIAN, SEAFOOD $$

17 🍴 Map p24, B2

The best of the beachfront restaurants on Legian's car-free strip, Mozarella serves Italian fare that's more authentic than most. Fresh fish also features; service is rather polished and there are various open-air areas for moonlit dining plus a more sheltered dining room. (www.mozzarella-resto.com; Maharta Bali Hotel, Jl Padma Utara; meals from 90,000Rp)

Made's Warung
INDONESIAN $$

18 🍴 Map p24, D7

Made's was the original tourist warung in Kuta and its Westernised Indonesian menu has been much copied. Classic

Nasi campur

CARLINA TETERIS/GETTY IMAGES ©

dishes such as *nasi campur* (rice served with side dishes) are served in an open-fronted setting that harks back to when Kuta's tourist hot spots were lit by gas lantern. (📞0361-755297; www.madeswarung.com; Jl Pantai Kuta; meals from 40,000Rp; ⏰8am-11pm)

Pantai
SEAFOOD $$

19 ✖ Map p24, C8

It's location, location, location here at this beachside bar and grill. The food is stock tourist (seafood, Indo classics, pasta etc) but the setting overlooking the ocean is idyllic. Each year it gets a bit more stylish and upscale but it still avoids pretence. Follow the beach path south past the big Ramada Bintang Bali resort. (📞0361-753196; Jl Wana Segara; meals 50,000-150,000Rp; ⏰8am-10pm)

Poppies Restaurant
INTERNATIONAL $$

20 ✖ Map p24, D7

Poppies was one of the first restaurants to be established in Kuta (Poppies Gang I is even named after it). It is popular for its lush garden setting, which feels slightly mysterious in a romantic way. The menu is upmarket Western, Thai and Balinese. The *rijstaffel* (selection of dishes served with rice) and seafood are popular. (📞0361-751059; www.poppiesbali. com; Poppies Gang I; mains 65,000-120,000Rp; ⏰8am-11pm)

Zanzibar
INTERNATIONAL $$

21 ✖ Map p24, A1

This popular patio fronts a busy strip at Double Six Beach. Sunset is prime time; the best views are from the tables on the 2nd-floor terrace. Dishes include the nasi family and the burger bunch. If it's crowded, the many nearby competitors will also do just fine. (📞0361-733529; Jl Arjuna; meals from 50,000Rp; ⏰8am-11pm)

Indo-National
SEAFOOD, INTERNATIONAL $$

22 ✖ Map p24, C3

This popular restaurant is home away from home for legions of happy fans. Grab a cold one with the rest of the crew. Then order the heaped-up grilled seafood platter. (📞0361-759883; Jl Padma 17; mains 50,000-100,000Rp; ⏰8am-11pm)

Local Life
Sunset Drinks on the Legian Beach Sand

Bali sunsets regularly explode in stunning displays of reds, oranges and purples. Sipping a cold one while watching this free show to the beat of the surf is the top activity at 6pm. In Legian, the best place for this is the strip of beach that starts north of Jl Padma and runs to the south end of Double Six Beach. Along this car-free stretch of sand you'll find genial young local guys with simple chairs and cheap, cold beer (20,000Rp).

Bali's wildest clubs cluster in an approximate 300m radius of the top-rated Sky Garden Lounge. The distinction between drinking and clubbing is blurry at best, with one morphing into another as the night wears on (or the morning comes up). Most bars are free to enter, and often have special drink promotions and 'happy hours' that run at various intervals until after midnight. Savvy partiers follow the specials from venue to venue and enjoy a massively discounted night out (club owners count on the drink specials to lure in punters who then can't be bothered to leave).

Bali club ambience ranges from the laid-back vibe of the surfer dives to high-concept nightclubs with long drink menus and hordes of prowling servers. Prostitution has proliferated at some Kuta clubs.

Drinking

Sky Garden Lounge
BAR, CLUB

 23 Map p24, D6

This multilevel palace of flash flirts with height restrictions from its rooftop bar where all of Kuta twinkles around you. Look for top DJs, a ground-level cafe and paparazzi-wannabes. Munchers can enjoy a long menu of bar snacks and meals, which most people pair with shots. Roam from floor to floor of this vertical playpen. (www.skygardenbali.com; Jl Legian 61; ⏰24hr)

Twice Bar
BAR

24 Map p24, C6

Kuta's best effort at an indie rock club, with all the grungy – and sweaty – feel you could hope for. (Poppies Gang II; ⏰7pm-2am)

Jenja
CLUB

25 Map p24, C1

A very slick, high-concept nightclub in the new TS Suites hotel. Spread over several levels, DJs rev it up with disco, R&B, funk, soul and more. The crowd is a mix of well-healed locals and expats. The restaurant serves upscale fare, good for sharing. (☎0361-882 7711; www.jenjabali.com; TS Suites, Jl Nakula 18; ⏰6pm-2am)

Velvet
BAR

26 Map p24, C6

The sunset views can't be beat at this large terrace bar and cafe at the beach end of the Beachwalk mall. On many nights the venue morphs into a club

after 10pm. (📞0361-2658 1405; www.
vhbali.com; Jl Pantai Kuta, Beachwalk, Level 3;
🕐11am-late)

Bounty   CLUB

27 🚇 Map p24, D6

Set on a faux sailing boat amid a mini-
mall of food and drink, the Bounty
is a vast open-air disco that humps,
thumps and pumps all night. Get down
on the poop deck to hip-hop, techno,
house and anything else the DJs come
up with. Foam parties, go-go dancers,
drag shows and cheap shots add to the
rowdiness. (www.bountydiscotheque.com; Jl
Legian; 🕐8pm-4am)

Shopping

Surfer Girl   SURF GEAR

28 🔒 Map p24, D6

A local legend, the winsome logo says
it all about this vast store for girls of all
ages. Clothes, gear, bikinis and plenty
of other stuff in every shade of bubble-
gum ever made. (www.surfer-girl.com; Jl
Legian 138; 🕐9am-10pm)

☑ Top Tip

Shopping in Kuta & Legian

Many people spend – literally – a
major part of their trip shopping.
Kuta has a vast concentration of
cheap stores, which can be charac-
terised by noting that the top-selling
Kuta souvenir is a bottle-opener in
the shape of a penis. Look for huge,
flashy surf-gear emporiums on Kuta
Sq and Jl Legian. As you head north
along the latter into Legian, the
quality of the shops improves and
you start finding cute little boutiques, especially past Jl Melasti. Jl
Arjuna is lined with wholesale fabric,
clothing and craft stores, giving it a
bazaar feel.

Rip Curl   SURF GEAR

29 🔒 Map p24, D6

Cast that mopey black stuff aside and
make a bit of a splash! Bali's largest
arm of the surfwear giant has a huge
range of beach clothes, waterwear and
surfboards. (📞0361-754238; www.ripcurl.
com; Jl Legian 62; 🕐9am-10pm)

Explore

Seminyak

Seminyak is where one talks about designers – or claims to be one. Bali's most posh shops can be found here, starting on Jl Raya Seminyak and Jl Raya Basangkasa, then spreading out from the curving spine of Jl Kayu Aya (Jl Laksmana) and Jl Petitenget. This is also where you'll find scores of top restaurants – from casually fun to attitudey outdoor lounges-slash-supper clubs.

The Region in a Day

☀ Start with a leisurely late breakfast at **Biku** (p39) or **Buzz Cafe** (p38). Then get yourself limbered up for the day ahead at one of Seminyak's many spas such as **Prana** (p38) or **Jari Menari** (p38). Wander over to **Seminyak Beach** (p37): feel the salty air and pause to ponder the offerings at **Pura Petitenget** (p37).

☀ Enjoy lunch at any of many casual spots that line Seminyak's restaurant row, Jl Kayu Aya. **Revolver** (p38) and **Ginger Moon** (p39) are but two examples. Now you're ready for one of Bali's highlights: shopping in Seminyak. Top options include **Theater Art Gallery** (p42) on Jl Raya Seminyak, **Bamboo Blonde** (p44) on Jl Kayu Aya, **White Peacock** (p43) on Jl Kayu Jati and **Bathe** (p42) on Jl Petitenget.

☾ Don't miss a spectacular sunset at trendy **Potato Head** (p41) or at one of the **beach bars** (p42) south of Jl Abimanyu. Dinner will swamp you with choices, but it's an easy walk across the sand to **La Lucciola** (p40) or inland at **Mama San** (p39). Later, party the hours away at **Mantra** (p41) or the spectacle that is **Bali Jo** (p39).

♥ Best of Bali

Beaches
Seminyak Beach (p37)

Nightlife
Potato Head (p41)

Mantra (p41)

Pampering
Prana (p38)

Jari Menari (p38)

Eating
Biku (p39)

Pura Petitenget (p39)

Shopping
Bamboo Blonde (p44)

Drifter (p43)

Gay Bali
Dix Club (p39)

Bali Jo (p39)

❶ Getting There & Around

🚖 **Taxi** Taxis from the airport will cost 60,000Rp to 90,000Rp.

Walk Jl Raya Seminyak and Jl Raya Basangkasa have decent walking. Unfortunately, Jl Kayu Aya, Jl Petitenget and Jl Drupadi spell pedestrian peril. Beware blind corners and chasms that can cause great injury. When possible, opt for the beach, a quick way to Kuta and Legian.

For reviews see

⊙ Experiences	p37
⊗ Eating	p38
⊜ Drinking	p41
⊕ Shopping	p42

0   500 m
0   0.25 miles

HOMER SYKES/GETTY IMAGES ©

Preparing temple offerings

Experiences

Seminyak Beach   BEACH

1 ⊙ Map p36, A2

A good stretch of Seminyak's beach is found near Pura Petitenget. It is usually uncrowded and has plenty of parking. It is often the scene of both religious ceremonies and surfing. Note that the stream to the north by Mano cafe is often unsavoury after rains. Insiders favour the patch of sand just south of Ku De Ta. Vendors will sell you cold beers for less than half what the club charges, yet you can still hear the throbbing soundtrack.

Enjoy sundowners on a fun strip of beach that runs south from the end of Jl Abimanyu to Jl Arjuna in Legian. The vendors are mellow and a sunset lounger and ice-cold Bintang costs about 15,000Rp. A **beach walk** makes wandering this stretch a breeze and you can choose from various beach bars.

Pura Petitenget   HINDU TEMPLE

2 ⊙ Map p36, A2

This is an important temple and the scene of many ceremonies. It is one of a string of sea temples that stretches from Pura Luhur Ulu Watu on the Bukit Peninsula north to Tanah Lot in western Bali. Petitenget loosely translates as 'magic box', a treasured belonging of the legendary 16th-century priest Nirartha, who refined the Balinese religion and visited this site often. (Jl Pantai Kaya Aya)

Jari Menari
SPA

3 Map p36, E3

Jari Menari is true to its name, which means 'dancing fingers': your body will be one happy dance floor. The all-male staff use massage techniques that emphasise rhythm. (0361-736740; www.jarimenari.com; Jl Raya Basangkasa 47; sessions from 350,000Rp; 9am-9pm)

Prana
SPA

4 Map p36, E3

A palatial Moorish fantasy that is easily the most lavishly decorated spa in Bali, Prana offers everything from basic hour-long massages to facials and all manner of beauty treatments. Feel internally cleansed after Ayurvedic treatments. (0361-730840; www.pranaspabali.com;

☑ Top Tip

Wrong Number?

Some of Bali's landline phone numbers (those with area codes that include 0361, across the south and Ubud) are being changed on an ongoing basis. To accommodate increased demand for lines, a digit is being added to the start of the existing six- or seven-digit phone numbers. So 0361-761 area code might become 0361-4761. The schedule and plans for the new numbers change regularly, but usually you'll hear a recording first in Bahasa Indonesian and then in English telling you which digit to add to the changed number.

Jl Kunti 118X; massages from 450,000Rp; 10am-10pm)

Bodyworks
SPA

5 Map p36, B2

Get waxed, get your hair done, get the kinks rubbed out of your joints – all this and more is on the menu at this uberpopular spa in the heart of Seminyak. (0361-733317; www.bodyworksbali.com; Jl Kayu Jati 2; massages from 260,000Rp; 9am-10pm)

Eating

Buzz Cafe
CAFE $

6 Map p36, E3

The name is eponymous at this busy cafe located behind some rare Seminyak trees right where Jl Kunti meets Jl Raya Seminyak. The open front lets you wave in fellow glitterati as they saunter past. The fresh drink of choice is the Green Hornet – a combo of lemon, lime and mint. (0818 350 444; Jl Raya Seminyak 99; mains from 30,000Rp; 7am-10pm;)

Revolver
CAFE $

7 Map p36, C2

Wander down a tiny *gang* (narrow alley) and push through narrow wooden doors to reach this matchbox of a coffee bar, which many claim has the best java, east of Java. There are just a few tables in the creatively retro room – nab one and enjoy tasty fresh bites for breakfast and lunch. (off Jl Kayu Aya; snacks from 20,000Rp; 7am-6pm;)

Biku
FUSION $$

8   Map p36, B1

Housed in an old shop that used to sell antiques, hugely popular Biku retains the timeless vibe of its predecessor. The menu combines Indonesian and other Asian and Western influences; book for lunch or dinner. Dishes, from the exquisite breakfasts and the elegant local choices to Bali's best burger, are artful and delicious. (📞0361-857 0888; www.bikubali.com; Jl Petitenget; meals 40,000-120,000Rp; 🕙8am-11pm; 🛜)

Mama San
FUSION $$

9   Map p36, D2

All the action is on the 2nd floor of this buzzy warehouse-sized restaurant. A long cocktail list provides liquid balm for the mojito set and has lots of tropical-flavoured pours. The menu emphasises small dishes from across Southeast Asia. (📞0361-730436; www.mamasanbali.com; Jl Raya Kerobokan 135; mains 80,000-200,000Rp; 🕙noon-11pm)

Petitenget
BISTRO $$

10   Map p36, A1

If it wasn't so hot, you could be in Paris. Soft jazz classics play at this very appealing bistro that mixes a casual terrace, bar and a more formal dining area. The menu has seasonal specials and features flavours of Europe and Asia. Everything is artfully prepared; there's a fun little kids menu. (📞0361-473 3054; www.petitenget.net; Jl Petitenget 40; breakfast mains 30,000-70,000Rp, lunch & dinner mains 50,000-200,000Rp; 🕙7am-10.30pm; 🛜)

Local Life
Gay Seminyak

A stretch of Seminyak's Jl Camplung Tanduk is the island's de facto gay bastion. A strip of small bars and clubs are filled with revellers most nights, with the crowds more mixed at some than others. **Bali Jo** (📞0361-847 5771; www.balijoebar.com; Jl Camplung Tanduk; 🕙3pm-3am; 🛜) is simply fun – albeit with falsies. Drag queens rock the house and the flamboyant shows draw crowds both inside and watching from out on the street. The name of freewheeling **Dix Club** (📞0878 6568 6615; Jl Camplung Tanduk; 🕙3pm-3am) says it all.

Earth Cafe & Market
CAFE $$

11   Map p36, D2

The good vibes are organic at this newly expanded vegetarian cafe and store amid the upmarket retail ghetto of Seminyak. Choose from creative salads, sandwiches or wholegrain vegan goodies. The beverage menu includes fresh juice mixes with serious names like 'bone builder', 'gas tonic' and 'party detox'. (📞0361-732805; www.earthcafe-bali.com; Jl Kayu Aya; mains from 40,000Rp; 🕙7am-11pm; 🛜📶)

Ginger Moon
ASIAN $$

12   Map p36, C2

Australian Dean Keddell was one of scores of young chefs lured to Bali to set up restaurants. His creation is a very appealing, airy space with carved wood and palms. The menu features a sort of 'Best of' list of favourites served in portions designed for sharing and grazing. (☎0361-734533; www.ginger-moonbali.com; Jl Kayu Aya 7; mains 70,000-160,000Rp; ☺11am-midnight; ❄ 🛜)

Rolling Fork ITALIAN $$

13 ✗ Map p36, E3

A little gnocchi-sized trattoria, Rolling Fork serves excellent Italian fare. Breakfast features gorgeous baked goods and excellent coffees. Lunch and dinner include authentic and tasty pastas, salads, seafood and more. The open-air dining room has an alluring retro charm; the Italian owners provide just the right accent. (☎0361-733 9633; Jl Kunti; mains from 60,000Rp; ☺8am-10pm)

Wacko Burger BURGERS $$

14 ✗ Map p36, B3

It's like you died and went to comfort-food heaven. The burgers here are beloved as are the onion rings, fries, shakes and more. There are all manner of toppings and condiments to choose from. It's located back from the road in a cheesy art-filled strip mall. (☎0361-739178; www.wackoburger.com; Jl Kayu Aya; mains from 50,000Rp; ☺noon-9.30pm)

Fat Gajah ASIAN $$

15 ✗ Map p36, D2

Noodles and dumplings rarely look this good. The open-front restaurant has a shaded terrace, while inside mirrors and dark wood give it a vintage colonial feel. Dishes are prepared with organic ingredients; dumplings come

✓ Top Tip

Where's Jl Oberoi?

Back in the day, roads in south Bali were often built to serve some tourist destination near the beach and took their names from the same. However, slowly but surely, what were once dirt trails are getting truly Balinese names as places such as Seminyak urbanise. So it is with the former Jl Oberoi (named after the luxe and highly recommended beachfront hotel), which now is called Jl Kayu Aya (after about a decade as Jl Laksmana) and is Seminyak's unofficial restaurant- and shop-lined main drag.

fried or steamed. (☎0361-868 8212; www.fatgajah.com; Jl Basangkasa 21; mains 50,000-80,000Rp; ☺8.30am-11pm)

Sate Bali INDONESIAN $$

Ignore the strip-mall location (see **14** ✗ Map p36, B3) and enjoy traditional Balinese dishes at this small cafe run by Nyoman Sudiyasa (who also has a cooking school here). The multicourse *rijstaffel* (selection of dishes served with rice) is a symphony of tastes. (☎0361-736734; Jl Kayu Aya; meals from 100,000Rp; ☺11am-10pm)

La Lucciola FUSION $$$

16 ✗ Map p36, A2

A sleek beachside restaurant with good views from the 2nd-floor tables across a lovely lawn and sand to the surf. The bar is big with sunset-watchers, although most then move onto dinner here. The menu is a creative melange of

Raw spring rolls

international fare with an Italian flair. (📞0361-730838; Jl Petitenget; mains 120,000-400,000Rp; ⏰9am-10pm)

Drinking

Potato Head

CLUB

17 📍 Map p36, A1

Bali's coolest beach club. Wander up off the sand or follow a long drive off Jl Petitenget and you'll discover a truly captivating creation on a grand scale. The clever design is striking and you'll find much to amuse, from an enticing pool to a swanky restaurant plus lots of loungers for chillin' the night away under the stars. (📞0361-473 7979; www.ptthead. com; Jl Petitenget; ⏰11am-2am; 🛜)

Mantra

LOUNGE

18 📍 Map p36, B1

Retro style meets tropical languor at this deservedly popular bar. There's a tree-shaded terrace out front that's the place to be late at night as dancing starts spontaneously. Inside the walls are lined with photos and art; there are regular special exhibits. Visiting DJs spin tunes and you can choose from creative drinks and snacks. (📞0361-473 7681; www.mantra bali.com; Jl Petitenget 77X; ⏰3pm-late)

Red Carpet Champagne Bar

BAR

19 📍 Map p36, D2

Choose from over 200 types of champagne at this over-the-top glam bar on

Seminyak's couture strip. Waltz the red carpet and toss back a few namesake flutes while contemplating a raw oyster and displays of frilly frocks. It's open to the street (but elevated, dahling) so you can gaze down on the masses. (📞0361-737889; www.redcarpetchampagnebar.com; Jl Kayu Aya 42; ⏰11am-late)

Ku De Ta   CLUB

20 📍 Map p36, B3

Ku De Ta teems with Bali's beautiful people (including those whose status is purely aspirational). Scenesters perfect their 'bored' look over drinks during the day, gazing at the fine stretch of beach. Sunset brings out crowds, who snatch a cigar at the bar or dine on eclectic fare at tables. The music throbs with increasing intensity through the night. (📞0361-736969; www.kudeta.net; Jl Kayu Aya 9; ⏰8am-late)

◯ Local Life
Cheap & Cheerful Sunset Drinks

Enjoy sundowners on a fun strip of beach that runs south from the end of Jl Camplung Tanduk to Jl Arjuna in Legian. The vendors here are mellow and a sunset lounger and ice-cold Bintang costs about 15,000Rp. A beach walk makes wandering this stretch a breeze and you can choose from various beach bars, including the Moorish fantasy of **La Plancha** (📞0361-730603; off Jl Camplung Tanduk; ⏰8am-midnight).

Ryoshi Seminyak House of Jazz   BAR

21 📍 Map p36, E4

The Seminyak branch of the local chain of Japanese restaurants has live jazz three nights a week on an intimate stage under a traditionally thatched roof. Expect some of the best local and visiting talent. (📞0361-731152; Jl Raya Seminyak 17; ⏰music from 8pm Mon, Wed & Fri)

Shopping

Bathe   BEAUTY, HOMEWARES

22 🔒 Map p36, B1

Double-down on your villa's romance with the handmade candles and bath salts at this shop that evoke the feel of a 19th-century French dispensary. You can't help but smile at the tub filled with rubber ducks. (📞0361-473 7580; www.bathe store.com; Jl Petitenget 100X; ⏰9am-8pm)

Vivacqua   ACCESSORIES

23 🔒 Map p36, E3

Bags of all shapes and sizes, from stylish ones you'll take to a top Kerobokan restaurant so you can filch a breadstick, to large ones ready to haul beach paraphernalia. (📞0361-736212; Jl Basangkasa 8; ⏰10am-6pm)

Theater Art Gallery   PUPPETS

24 🔒 Map p36, E4

Newly expanded, specialises in vintage and reproduction puppets used in traditional Balinese theatre. Just looking at the animated faces peering back at you is a delight. (Jl Raya Seminyak; ⊙9am-8pm)

Ashitaba
HANDICRAFTS

25 🔒 Map p36, E3

Tenganan, the Aga village of east Bali, produces the intricate and beautiful rattan items sold here. Containers, bowls, purses and more (from 50,000Rp) display the very fine weaving. (Jl Raya Seminyak 6; ⊙9am-8pm)

Paul Ropp
CLOTHING

26 🔒 Map p36, D2

The elegant main shop for one of Bali's premier high-end fashion designers for men and women. Most goods are made in the hills above Denpasar. And what goods they are – rich silks and cottons, vivid to the point of gaudy, with hints of Ropp's roots in the tie-dyed 1960s. (☑0361-735613; www.paulropp.com; Jl Kayu Aya; ⊙9am-9pm)

Lulu Yasmine
WOMEN'S CLOTHING

27 🔒 Map p36, D2

Designer Luiza Chang gets inspiration from her worldwide travels for her elegant line of clothes. (☑0361-736763; www.luluyasmine.com; Jl Kayu Aya; ⊙9am-9pm)

Drifter
SURF GEAR

28 🔒 Map p36, C2

High-end surf fashion, surfboards, gear, books and brands such as Obey and Wegener. Started by two savvy

✅ Top Tip
Whining About Wine
An insane amount of taxes and duties levied on alcohol brought into Indonesia means that a so-so bottle of Australian plonk can cost A$40 in a shop and A$60 or more in a restaurant. Local – and cheap – vintages have few fans so if you want to enjoy a tipple instead of (actually quite good) Bintang beer, you'll need to bring some with you. Visitors to Bali can bring in 1L of alcohol, so practically speaking, make certain everybody in your group has a bottle in their bags.

surfer dudes, the shop stocks goods noted for their individuality and high quality. There's also a small cafe and a patio. (☑0361-733274; www.driftersurf.com; Jl Kayu Aya 50; ⊙9am-9pm)

Kendra Gallery
GALLERY

29 🔒 Map p36, D3

This high-end gallery has shows that are thoughtfully and creatively curated. Has regular special events. (☑0361-736628; www.kendragallery.com; Jl Drupadi 88B; ⊙10am-7pm)

White Peacock
HOMEWARES

30 🔒 Map p36, B2

Styled like a country cottage, this is the place for cute cushions, throw rugs, table linens and more. (☑0361-733238; Jl Kayu Jati 1; ⊙9am-8pm)

Local Life
Seminyak Shopping

The shopping scene here is constantly changing: new boutiques appear, old ones vanish, some change into something else while others move up the food chain. Seminyak shops could occupy days of your holiday. Designer boutiques, slick galleries, wholesale emporiums and family-run workshops are just some of the choices.

The interesting retail action picks up going north from the junction with Jl Arjuna where Jl Legian morphs into Jl Raya Seminyak and Jl Raya Basangkasa. The hunt gets especially ripe north of Jl Camplung Tanduk. Shopping peaks along Jl Kayu Aya and Jl Kayu Jati, and on into Kerobokan along Jl Petitenget.

Namu   CLOTHING

31 🔒 Map p36, B1

Designer Paola Zancanaro creates comfy and casual resortwear for men and women that doesn't take a holiday from style. The fabrics are lusciously tactile; many are hand-painted silk. (📞0361-279 7524; www.namustore.com; Jl Petitenget 23X; ⏰9am-8pm)

Indivie   HANDICRAFTS

32 🔒 Map p36, E3

The works of young designers based in Bali are showcased at this intriguing and glossy boutique. (📞0361-730927; www.indivie.com; Jl Raya Seminyak, Made's Warung; ⏰9am-9pm)

Divine Diva   WOMEN'S CLOTHING

33 🔒 Map p36, D2

A simple shop filled with Bali-made breezy styles for larger figures. One customer told us: 'It's the essence of agelessness.' You can custom order from the onsite tailors. (📞0361-732393; www.divinedivabali.com; Jl Kayu Aya 1A; ⏰9am-7pm)

Bamboo Blonde   WOMEN'S CLOTHING

34 🔒 Map p36, C2

Shop for frilly, sporty or sexy frocks and formal wear at this cheery designer boutique. (📞0361-731864; www.bambooblonde.com; Jl Kayu Aya 61; ⏰9am-9pm)

Niconico   CLOTHING

35 🔒 Map p36, B2

German designer Nico Genge has a line of intimate clothing, resortwear and swimwear that eschews glitz for a slightly more subtle look. Among his many Seminyak shops, this one has both the full collection and an art gallery upstairs. (📞0361-738875; Jl Kayu Aya; ⏰9am-9pm)

Biasa   CLOTHING

36 🔒 Map p36, E4

This is Bali-based designer Susanna Perini's premier shop. Her line of elegant tropicalwear for men and women combines cottons, silks and embroidery. The outlet store is at Jl Basangkasa 47. (📞0361-730308; www.biasabali.com; Jl Raya Seminyak 36; ⏰9am-9pm)

LONELY PLANET/GETTY IMAGES ©

Lily Jean boutique

Blue Glue Outlet   WOMEN'S CLOTHING

37 🔒 Map p36, E3

Bikinis from the hot local design shop at prices as small as their coverage. (Jl Basangkasa; ⏰9am-8pm)

Lily Jean   WOMEN'S CLOTHING

38 🔒 Map p36, C2

Saucy knickers underpin sexy women's clothing; most are Bali-made. This popular shop has flash digs in fashion's ground zero. It has another plant-covered outlet for simple cottonwear nearby. (📞0811 398 272; www.lily-jean.com; Jl Kayu Aya; ⏰10am-8pm)

Milo's   CLOTHING

39 🔒 Map p36, B2

The legendary local designer of silk finery has a lavish shop in the heart of designer row. Look for batik-bearing, eye-popping orchid patterns. (📞0361-822 2008; www.milos-bali.com; Jl Kayu Aya 992; ⏰10am-8pm)

Ganesha Bookshop   BOOKS

In a corner of the fabulous Biku restaurant (see 8 ✖ Map p36, B1), this tiny branch of Bali's best bookstore up in Ubud has all manner of local and literary treats. (Jl Petitenget; ⏰8am-11pm)

Explore

Kerobokan & Canggu

Kerobokan can rightly be called Seminyak North. Jl Petitenget seamlessly links the pair and, like its southern neighbour, Kerobokan has an ever-more alluring collection of shops and some of Bali's very best restaurants. This is also ground zero for private villa rentals, with walled compounds stretching west along the coast, past villa-dotted Canggu to the rugged surf and idyll pleasures of Echo Beach.

The Region in a Day

☀ Start off your day with you! Try some yoga at **Desa Seni** (p52) or a new look at **Amo Beauty Spa** (p52). Go for an invigorating ride on the surf breaks at **Batu Bolong Beach** (p51). Or just lighten your wallet while filling the carry-on at any of the many fine housewares stores such as **Hobo** (p57). Save money *and* space at the kid-friendly **JJ Bali Button** (p57).

☀ Kerobokan has a number of simple warungs that showcase Indonesian foods in settings visitors will enjoy; try **Warung Sulawesi** (p53) or the upscale **Merah Putih** (p55). For the afternoon, find your perfect spot of sand at the ever-more-popular **Batubelig Beach** (p51) or **Echo Beach** (p51), where you'll find sunbed and drink vendors. Or go for one of the less-visited stretches of sand on either side of Batu Bolong Beach.

☾ Look for a venue that grabs your fancy and enjoy sunset views at Batubelig Beach, just west of Kerobokan. Then don your nice duds and choose from some of Bali's best drinking and dining at **Sardine** (p56) or **Sarong** (p56), or try tasty **Warung Eny** (p53).

For a local's day in Kerobokan & Canggu see p48.

◯ Local Life

Beach Walk: Batubelig to Echo Beach (p48)

♥ Best of Bali

Surf Breaks
Echo Beach (p51)

Beaches
Batu Bolong Beach (p51)

Pampering
Desa Seni (p52)

Amo Beauty Spa (p52)

Eating
Sardine (p56)

Merah Putih (p55)

Warung Sulawesi (p53)

Shopping
JJ Bali Button (p57)

Hobo (p57)

For Kids
Gusto Gelato & Coffee (p52)

Canggu Club (p52)

❶ Getting There & Around

🚖 **Taxi** Taxis from the airport will cost 80,000Rp to 120,000Rp.

This area is quite spread out; even walks to the beach might be 2km or more. Renting a scooter, taking a taxi or getting rides from your villa driver will be necessary. Echo Beach has a taxi stand.

Local Life
Beach Walk: Batubelig to Echo Beach

Getting There

🚕 **Taxi** Getting to Batubelig is easy by cab. Echo Beach has its own taxi drivers so getting a ride back is also easy.

Walking the beach, it's only 4km from Batubelig Beach to Echo Beach, compared with a long circuitous drive inland. You'll cover stretches of empty sand and ford streams with only the roar of the surf for company. A few villages, temples, villas and simple cafes provide interest away from the water. You'll get wet on this walk; bring a waterproof bag for valuables.

❶ Batubelig Beach

Start this walk at one of the beach bars and cafes along Batubelig Beach. Get your fluids in for an adventure that can take anywhere from an hour to half a day depending on your whim. Look northwest along the beach and you can see the developments at Echo Beach in the distance.

❷ Water Crossing

The biggest obstacle on this entire walk is only about 500m from the start. The river and lagoon here flow into the ocean, often at a depth of 1m but at times not at all. However, after rains it may be much deeper and you'll decide not to swim the current: in this case, take the cool little footbridge over the lagoon to a couple of cafes, where you can call for a taxi.

❸ Berewa Beach

Greyish Berewa Beach, secluded among rice fields and villas, is about 2km up the sand from Seminyak (where you can also begin this walk). There are a couple of surfer cafes by the pounding sea; the grey volcanic sand here slopes steeply into foaming water. Look along the sand's edge for the vast Marabito Art Villa, a private estate that's an architectural wonder.

❹ Prancak Beach

Almost 1km further on you'll come to another (shallow) water crossing that also marks the large complex of **Pura Dalem Prancak**. A vendor or two may offer drinks on Pantai Prancak;

turn around facing the way you've come and you can see the sweep of the beach all the way to the airport.

❺ Nelayan Beach

A collection of fishing boats and huts marks this very mellow stretch of sand that lacks easy access to villa-land just inland.

❻ Batu Bolong Beach

Sometimes called Canggu Beach, hip and popular Batu Bolong Beach boasts the large Pura Batumejan complex with a striking pagoda-like temple. There are surfboard rentals, cafes and a fun mix of locals, expats and visitors.

❼ Echo Beach

Construction along the shore means you've reached Echo Beach (Pantai Batu Mejan), where you can reward yourself for your adventurous walk at the many cafes. A flock of shops means you can replace any clothes that are drenched beyond repair. Otherwise, take your camera out of its waterproof bag and nab shots of the popular surf break.

❽ Pererenan Beach

Yet to be found by the right developer, Pererenan Beach is the one for you, if you want your sand windswept and your waves unridden. It's an easy 300m further on from Echo Beach by sand and rock formations. There's a couple of good cafes here that don't have the crowds of Echo Beach.

JI Raya Kerobokan

SEMER

JI Raya Semer

E

27 🔲

24 🔲 ❌ 8

JI Raya Mertanadi

❌ 13

❌ 26

JI Raya Kerobokan

UMALA
KANGIN

17 20 4 ❌

Sundari
Day Spa

KUWUM

JI Umalas

D

JI Petitenget

❌ 9

JI Batubelig

KEROBOKAN 14

21 ❌ ❌
⚫ 6

Amo
Beauty
Spa

16 ❌

19 ❌

❌ 23

❌ 22

7 Canggu
Club

JI Pantai Berawa

Batubelig
Beach 2

C

10 ❌

11 ❌

CANGGU

Desa
5 ⚫
Seni

JI Pantai Berawa

JI Pemelisan Agung

B

25 🔲

JI Nelayan

JI Subak Catur

JI Pantai Batu Bolong

❌ 18

1 ❌

Batu
Bolong
Beach

Echo
Beach

3 ⚫

❌ 15

12 ❌

Teluk
Kuta

For reviews see

⚫ Experiences   p51
❌ Eating   p52
🔴 Drinking   p57
🔲 Shopping   p57

1 km
0.5 miles

Ⓝ

A   B   C   D   E

1

2

3

4

GERARD WALKER/GETTY IMAGES ©

Desa Seni (p52)

Experiences

Batu Bolong Beach   BEACH

1 ⊚ Map p50, A2

The beach at Batu Bolong is the most popular in the Canggu area. There's almost always a good mix of locals, expats and visitors hanging out in the cafes, surfing the breaks or watching it all from the sand. It's a classic beach scene, with rental umbrellas and loungers available. You can rent surfboards (100,000Rp per day) and take lessons. Overlooking it all is the centuries-old **Pura Batumejan** complex with a striking pagoda-like temple.

Taxis here can take you around the Canggu area (50,000Rp) or to more distant points like Seminyak (100,000Rp).

Batubelig Beach   BEACH

2 ⊚ Map p50, C4

The sand narrows here but there are some good places for a drink, both grand and simple. Easily reached via Jl Batubelig, this is a good place to start a walk along the curving sands northwest to the popular beaches as far as Echo Beach.

Echo Beach   BEACH

3 ⊚ Map p50, A1

Surfers and those who watch them flock here for the high-tide left-hander that regularly tops 2m. The greyish sand right in front of the developments can vanish at high tide, but you'll find wide strands both east and west. Batu Bolong beach is 500m east. (Pantai Batu Mejan)

Sundari Day Spa
SPA

4 ⦿ Map p50, E3

This lovely spa strives to offer the services of a five-star resort without the high prices. The massage oils and other potions are organic and there's a full menu of therapies and treatments on offer. (📞0361-735073; www.sundari-dayspa. com; Jl Petitenget 7; massages from 230,000Rp; ⏱9am-8pm)

Desa Seni
YOGA

5 ⦿ Map p50, C3

Desa Seni comprises classic wooden homes that have been transformed into a luxurious hotel. It is also renowned for its wide variety of yoga classes, which are offered daily and have a large following among local expats and nonguests. (📞0361-844 6392; www.desaseni.com; Jl Kayu Putih 13; classes from 140,000Rp; ⏱varies)

☑️ Top Tip

Best Time for Tanah Lot

Just west of Echo Beach, Pura Tanah Lot is a heavily touristed temple right on the ocean. Although picturesque, much of its structure, which sits on rocks amid the surf, is of recent construction. The scores of souvenir-sellers jamming the site, coupled with the nightmarish traffic jams for sunset-viewing, make a visit anything but serene. For a much more pleasant experience, drop by in the morning when the atmosphere is somnolent.

Amo Beauty Spa
SPA

6 ⦿ Map p50, D4

With some of Asia's top models lounging about it feels like you've stepped into the studios of *Vogue*. Besides massages, other services range from hair care to pedicures and unisex waxing. (📞0361-275 3337; www.amospa.com; 100 Jl Petitenget; massages from 180,000Rp; ⏱9am-9pm)

Canggu Club
HEALTH & FITNESS

7 ⦿ Map p50, C2

Bali's expats shuttlecock themselves silly at the Canggu Club, a New Age version of something you'd expect to find during the Raj. The vast, perfectly virescent lawn is manicured for croquet. Get sweaty with tennis, squash, polo, cricket, the spa or the 25m pool. Many villa rentals include guest passes here. The garish new Splash Waterpark is hugely popular. (📞0361-844 6385; www. cangguclub.com; Jl Pantai Berawa; adult/child day pass 240,000/120,000Rp; 📶)

Eating

Gusto Gelato & Coffee
ICECREAM $

8 ✖️ Map p50, E4

Bali's best gelato is made fresh through the day and served to throngs looking to lick something cool and refreshing. The flavours pop; enjoy a coffee drink in the back garden. (📞0361-552 2190; www.gusto-gelateria.com; Jl Raya Mertanadi 46; treats from 15,000Rp; ⏱10am-9pm Mon-Sat; ❄️📶)

Local Life
Kerobokan's Favourite Warung

Although seemingly upscale, Kerobokan is blessed with many a fine place for a local meal. One of the favourites is **Warung Sulawesi** (Jl Petitenget; meals from 30,000Rp; ⊘10am-6pm). Here you'll find a table in a quiet family compound and enjoy fresh Balinese and Indonesian food served in classic warung style. Choose a rice, then pick from a captivating array of dishes that are always at their peak at noon. The long beans – yum!

Warung Eny
INDONESIAN $

9 🍴 Map p50, D4

The eponymous Eny cooks everything herself at this tiny open-front warung nearly hidden behind various potted plants. Look for the roadside sign that captures the vibe: 'The love cooking.' Seafood such as large prawns smothered in garlic are delicious and most ingredients are organic. Ask about her fun cooking classes. (📞0361-473 6892; Jl Petitenget; mains from 35,000Rp; ⊘8am-10pm)

Green Ginger
ASIAN $

10 🍴 Map p50, C2

A profusion of flowering plants, art and eccentric bits of furniture mark this cool little boho cafe on the fast-changing strip in Canggu. The menu has fresh and tasty vegetarian and noodle dishes from across Asia. (📞0878 6211 2729; Jl Pantai Berawa; meals from 30,000Rp; ⊘8am-9.30pm; ✐)

Indotopia
ASIAN $

11 🍴 Map p50, C2

Otherwise known as 'Warung Vietnam', the bowls of *pho* here are simply superb. Lots of rich beefy goodness contrasting with perfect noodles and fragrant greens. Prefer something sweeter? Go for the Saigon banana crêpes. (📞0822 3773 7760; Jl Pantai Berawa 34; mains from 30,000Rp; ⊘8am-10pm; 📶)

Mandira Cafe
CAFE $

12 🍴 Map p50, A1

Although Echo Beach is rapidly going upscale, this classic surfers' dive has battered picnic tables with front-row seats for surfing action. Quaff a cheap Bintang while you Instagram the best action out on the breaks. The timeless menu includes jaffles, banana pancakes, club sandwiches and smoothies. (Jl Pura Batu Mejan; meals 25,000-50,000Rp; ⊘8am-10pm; 📶)

Fruit Market
MARKET $

13 🍴 Map p50, E3

Bali's numerous climate zones (hot and humid near the ocean, cool and dry up the volcano slopes) mean that pretty much any fruit or vegetable can be grown within the island's small confines. Vendors here sell them all, including lesser known fruits such as nubby mangosteens. A string of stalls prepares assorted tasty snacks and there's a small night market. (cnr Jl Raya Kerobokan & Jl Gunung Tangkuban Perahu; ⊘7am-10pm)

Understand

The Villa Life

Like temple offerings after a ceremony, villas can be found across south Bali, with the greatest concentration in Kerobokan and Canggu. They're often built in the middle of rice paddies, seemingly overnight. The villa boom has been quite controversial for environmental, aesthetic and economic reasons (many skip collecting government taxes from guests).

Villas can be bacchanal retreats for groups of friends who share multiple bedrooms set around a pool. Others are smaller, more intimate and part of larger developments. Expect a private garden and pool (which can range in size from plunge to substantial), a kitchen (you can usually arrange for a cook if you want to eat in your compound), air-con bedrooms and an open-air common space.

Also potentially included are your own staff (cook, driver, cleaner) or at least staff shared with a few units, lush grounds, private beachfront, isolation (which can be good or bad – Canggu, for example, can be isolated by traffic) and wi-fi.

After dark, some villa walls hide surprises. On any night in Kerobokan and Canggu there are a few private parties going on that are a bit bigger than your average kegger in a backyard. Many feature top DJs and an attitude-heavy list of visiting (self-professed) celebrities and the like. Getting an invite to one of these soirées is rather elusive, although on occasion uninvited guests turn up in the form of police, who invariably make a few arrests for drugs.

Renting a Villa

Rates range from under US$200 per night for a modest villa to US$1200 per night and beyond for your own tropical estate. There are often deals, especially in the low season, and several couples sharing can make something grand affordable. Recommended agents include **Bali Discovery** (✆0361-286 283; www.balidiscovery.com), **Bali Private Villas** (✆0361-316 6455; www.baliprivatevillas.com) and **Bali Tropical Villas** (✆0361-732 083; www.balitropical-villas.com).

Some things to keep in mind and ask about when renting a villa: How far is the villa from the beach and shops? Is a driver or car service included? If there is a cook, is food included? Is laundry included?

LUCIA TERUI/GETTY IMAGES ©

Pura Tanah Lot (p52)

Merah Putih

INDONESIAN $$

14 Map p50, D4

Merah Putih means 'red and white', which are the colours of the Indonesian flag. That's perfect for this excellent restaurant that celebrates food from across the archipelago. The short menu is divided between traditional and modern – the latter combining Indo flavours with diverse foods. The soaring dining room has a hip style and the service is excellent. (☏0361-846 5950; www. merahputihbali.com; Jl Petitenget 100X; mains 60,000-150,000Rp; ⊗noon-3pm & 6-11pm)

Beach House

CAFE $$

15 Map p50, A1

Face the Echo Beach waves from stylish loungers or chill on a variety of couches and picnic tables. Enjoy the menu of breakfasts, salads, grilled fare and tasty dishes such as calamari with aioli. Evening barbecues are popular – especially on Sunday – and feature fresh seafood, steaks and live music. (☏0361-747 4604; www.echobeachhouse.com; Jl Pura Batu Mejan; mains 40,000-110,000Rp; ⊗8am-10pm; 🛜)

Warung Sobat

SEAFOOD $$

16 Map p50, D3

Set in a sort of bungalow-style brick courtyard, this old-fashioned restaurant excels at fresh Balinese seafood with an

Italian accent (lots of garlic!). First-time visitors feel like they've made a discovery, and if you have the sensational lobster platter (a bargain at 350,000Rp for two; order in advance), you will too. Book. (📞0361-473 8922; Jl Batubelig 11; mains 30,000-150,000Rp; ⏰noon-11pm; 📶)

Old Man's   BURGERS, INTERNATIONAL $$

18 🍴 Map p50, A2

You'll have a tough time deciding just where to sit down to enjoy your beer at this vast open-air joint back off Batu Bolong beach. The menu is aimed at surfers and surfer-wannabes: burgers, pizza, fish and chips, and for the New Age surfers: salads. On many nights

Local Life
Canggu's Cafes

In the meandering roads of the Canggu area, set among villas and rice fields, are an ever-growing collection of interesting and creative cafes. Start your day over coffee or have a quick, tasty lunch or a post-beach refresher. **Monsieur Spoon** (Jl Pantai Batu Bolong; snacks from 20,000Rp; ⏰6am-9pm; ❄) has excellent baked goods, while **Betelnut Cafe** (📞0821 4680 7233; Jl Pantai Batu Bolong; mains from 45,000Rp; ⏰7am-10pm; ❄📶) has a hip vibe drawn right from Batu Bolong Beach. **Bungalow** (📞0361-844 6567; Jl Pantai Berawa; mains from 30,000Rp; ⏰8am-6pm; ❄), in the heart of Canggu, is an appealing place to linger over a fresh juice.

there's live music (think classic rock). (📞0361-846 9158; Jl Pantai Batu Bolong; mains from 50,000Rp; ⏰8am-midnight)

Naughty Nuri's   INDONESIAN $$

19 🍴 Map p50, C3

Inspired by the overhyped Ubud original, this Nuri's is simply overcrowded. Remarkably, it has become a must-see stop for tourists from across Indonesia, who tuck into the American-style fare such as 'ribs with wonderment'. The original's trademark kick-arse martinis remain on the menu. Queues often form for tables and watching the tourists watch each other is actually rather fun. (📞0361-847 6722; Jl Batubelig 41; meals from 50,000Rp; ⏰11am-10.30pm)

Sardine   SEAFOOD $$$

20 🍴 Map p50, E3

Seafood fresh from the famous Jimbaran market is the star at this elegant yet intimate, casual yet stylish restaurant in a beautiful bamboo pavilion that is ably presided over by Pascal and Pika Chevillot. Open-air tables overlook a private rice field patrolled by Sardine's own flock of ducks. (📞0361-843 6111; www.sardinebali.com; Jl Petitenget 21; meals US$20-50; ⏰11.30am-11pm)

Sarong   FUSION $$$

21 🍴 Map p50, D4

Usually open to the evening breezes, the dining room has plush furniture and gleaming place settings that twinkle in the candlelight. But opt for tables out the back where you can let the stars do the twinkling. The food spans the globe; small plates are popular with those wishing to pace an evening enjoying the commodious bar. No children allowed. (☎0361-473 7809; www.sarongbali.com; Jl Petitenget 19X; mains 150,000-350,000Rp; ⏱5-11pm)

Drinking

Pantai

BAR

22 🚇 Map p50, C4

The authorities regularly bulldoze away the impromptu drinking shacks that appear along this inviting stretch of beach just north of the W hotel. But Pantai has so far had more lives than a cat and stubbornly keeps offering up cheap drinks, mismatched tables and splendid surf and sunset views. (Batubelig Beach; ⏱9am-9pm)

Mozaic Beach Club

CLUB

23 🚇 Map p50, C4

The original Mozaic restaurant in Ubud is renowned for its fanatical attention to detail and that tradition continues at this beautiful beachside club. You can lounge around the elegant pool or wander the elaborate multilevel restaurant and bar. It's never quite as crowded as you think it should be, and daily drink specials include free tapas. (☎0361-473 5796; www.mozaic-beachclub.com; Jl Pantai Batubelig; meals from 150,000Rp; ⏱10am-1am)

Shopping

JJ Bali Button

ARTS & CRAFTS

24 🔒 Map p50, E3

Zillions of beads and buttons made from shells, plastic, metal and more are displayed in what initially looks like a candy store. Elaborately carved wooden buttons are 700Rp. (Jl Gunung Tangkuban Perahu; ⏱9am-7pm)

Dylan Board Store

SURFBOARDS

25 🔒 Map p50, B1

Famed big-wave rider Dylan Longbottom runs this custom surfboard shop. A talented shaper, he creates boards for novices and pros alike. He also stocks plenty of his designs ready to go. (☎0857 3853 7402; Jl Pantai Batu Bolong; ⏱noon-6pm)

Hobo

HOMEWARES

26 🔒 Map p50, E4

Elegance mixes with quirky at this enticing shop filled with gifts and housewares, most of which can slip right into your carry-on bag. (☎0361-733369; www.thehobostore.com; Jl Raya Kerobokan 105; ⏱9am-8pm)

Bambooku

HOMEWARES

27 🔒 Map p50, E4

House linens made from bamboo are the speciality at this tidy shop. The fabric is amazingly soft and is much sought after by people with allergies. A set of sheets and pillowcases for a double bed costs 1,800,000Rp. (☎0361-780 7836; www.bambooku.com; Jl Raya Mertanadi; ⏱9am-7pm)

Top Experiences
Feeling Spiritual at Pura Luhur Batukau

Getting There

🚗 **Car** You'll need to charter a car and driver for the day. Getting here from south Bali can take one to two hours, depending on traffic.

One of the island's holiest and most underrated temples, Pura Luhur Batukau makes for an excellent day trip and is the most spiritual temple you can easily visit. It is surrounded by forest, the atmosphere is cool and misty, and the chants of priests are backed by singing birds. The temple is near the base of Gunung Batukau, the island's second-highest mountain (2276m) and the third of Bali's three major volcanoes. Nearby, you can drive through the lushly iconic Jatiluwih rice fields.

Jatiluwih rice fields

Don't Miss

Pura Luhur Batukau

Within the temple complex, look for the seven-roofed *meru* dedicated to Maha Dewa, the mountain's guardian spirit, as well as shrines for Bratan, Buyan and Tamblingan lakes. The main *meru* in the inner courtyard have little doors shielding small ceremonial items. It's impossible to ignore the deeply spiritual mood.

Facing the temple, take a short walk around to the left to see a small white-water stream where the air resonates with tumbling water. Get here early for the best chance of seeing the dark and foreboding slopes of the volcano.

Gunung Batukau

From Pura Luhur Batukau you can climb Gunung Batukau. To trek to the top of the 2276m peak, you'll need a guide, which can be arranged at the temple. Expect to pay 1,000,000Rp (for two people) for an arduous journey that will take at least seven hours one way. The rewards are amazing views alternating with thick, dripping jungle.

Jatiluwih Rice Fields

At Jatiluwih, which means 'truly marvellous', you will be rewarded with vistas of centuries-old rice terraces that exhaust your ability to describe green. Emerald ribbons curve around the hill-sides, stepping back as they climb to the blue sky.

The terraces are emblematic of Bali's ancient rice-growing culture. Stop along the narrow, twisting 18km road and follow the water as it runs through channels and bamboo pipes from one plot to the next.

admission to Pura Luhur Batukau: 10,000Rp donation

☑ Top Tips

▸ Sashes and sarongs are provided.

▸ Admire the many forms of offerings from a few flower petals in a banana leaf to vastly elaborate affairs that can feed many gods.

▸ A two-hour mini-jaunt up Batukau costs 200,000Rp.

▸ There is a road toll for Jatiluwih visitors (15,000Rp per person, plus 5000Rp per car).

▸ Much of the rice you'll see is traditional, rather than the hybrid versions grown elsewhere on the island. Look for heavy short husks of red rice.

✖ Take a Break

There are a couple of simple cafes for refreshments along the Jatiluwih drive. They are nothing fancy but you're there for the views.

Explore

Jimbaran

For many, Jimbaran means a wonderful grilled seafood dinner over-looking the serene bay from tables on the sand. By day, Jimbaran has two markets that bustle with business as Bali's rich stocks of fish, fruits and vegetables are bought and sold. The sweeping crescent of sand fronting the bay is a fine alternative to venturing further along the Bukit Peninsula.

The Region in a Day

☀ Waking with the sun in Jimbaran will be rewarded when you visit the frenetic world of the **Fish Market** (p63), as well as the fruit and vegetable wonderland that is the **Morning Market** (p63). For a pause, you might try a cafe in one of the resorts that are discreetly set back from the beach.

☀ Your afternoon should be all about Jimbaran's excellent **beach** (p63). Stroll its 4km and find a good shady spot to relax on a rented sun lounger. Despite rumours of future plans, the area is not yet overwhelmed with hotels and resorts, so you won't find the sands crowded.

☾ As the sun creates its spectacular vermilion theatrics in the west, wander through the fragrant smoke of the three main areas of seafood warungs to find your spot for dinner. The fish is always fresh from the market and you can choose from what's on offer in huge tanks and beds of ice before it goes on the flaming coconut-shell-fuelled grills.

♥ **Best of Bali**

Eating

Lei Lei Seaside Barbeque (p64)

Warung Bamboo (p64)

❶ Getting There & Around

🚗 **Taxi** From Kuta a taxi will cost 50,000Rp and from Seminyak about 80,000Rp. Traffic on the main road past the airport can get clogged, leading to very long delays.

Walk You can easily walk Jimbaran's beach to browse the seafood warungs and market.

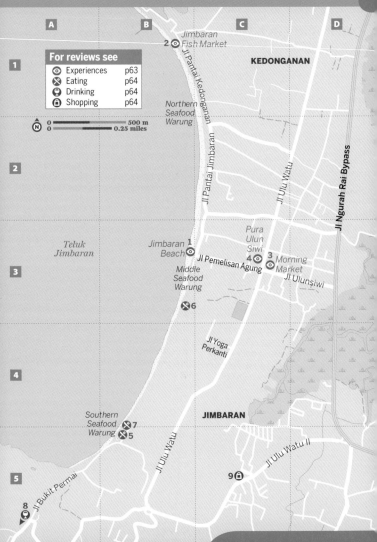

A   B   C   D

KEDONGANAN

2 ◉ *Jimbaran Fish Market*

Jl Pantai Kedonganan

Northern Seafood Warung

For reviews see	
◉ Experiences	p63
✖ Eating	p64
⊖ Drinking	p64
🔒 Shopping	p64

N   0   500 m
     0   0.25 miles

Jl Pantai Jimbaran

Jl Ulu Watu

Jl Ngurah Rai Bypass

Teluk Jimbaran

Pura Ulun Siwi

Jimbaran Beach 1 ◉
Jl Pemelisan Agung

4 ◉ 3 ◉ *Morning Market*
Jl Ulunsiwi

Middle Seafood Warung

✖ 6

Jl Yoga Perkanti

JIMBARAN

Southern Seafood Warung ✖ 7
✖ 5

Jl Ulu Watu

Jl Ulu Watu II

9 🔒

8 ⊖
Jl Bukit Permai

Jimbaran Beach

Experiences

Jimbaran Beach   BEACH

1 Map p62, B3

One of Bali's best beaches, Jimbaran's 4km-long arc of sand is mostly clean and there is no shortage of places to get a snack, a drink, a seafood dinner or to rent a sun lounger. The bay is protected by an unbroken coral reef, which keeps the surf more mellow than at Kuta, although you can still get breaks that are fun for bodysurfing.

Jimbaran Fish Market   MARKET

2 Map p62, B1

A popular morning stop on Bukit Peninsula ambles is this smelly, lively and frenetic fish market – just watch where you step. Brightly painted boats bob along the shore while huge cases of everything from small sardines to fearsome langoustines are hawked. The action is fast and furious. (Jimbaran Beach; ⏰6am-3pm)

Morning Market   MARKET

3 Map p62, C3

This is one of the best markets in Bali for a visit because: a) it's compact, so you can see a lot without wandering forever; b) local chefs swear by the quality of the fruits and vegetables (ever seen a cabbage that big?); and c) they're used to tourists trudging about. (JI Ulu Watu; ☉6am-noon)

Pura Ulun Siwi
HINDU TEMPLE

4 ◉ Map p62, C3

Across from the morning market, this ebony-hued temple from the 18th century is a snoozy place until it explodes with life, offerings, incense and more on a holy day. (JI Ulu Watu)

Eating

Lei Lei Seaside Barbeque
SEAFOOD $$

5 ✕ Map p62, B5

An especially cheery outpost, with sparkling tanks filled with future taste-treats. The furniture here is slightly nicer than elsewhere. (✆0361-703296; off JI Bukit Permai; meals 80,000-200,000Rp; ☉noon-10pm)

Top Tip

Surfing

Jimbaran is a good place to access the very popular surf breaks off the airport. Head up the beach looking for a fishing boat (if you have a board, skippers will find you) and negotiate to be taken out to the breaks. Prices are very negotiable: 50,000Rp for a one-way trip is a good place to start.

Warung Bamboo
SEAFOOD $$

6 ✕ Map p62, B3

Warung Bamboo is slightly more appealing than its neighbours, all of which have a certain raffish charm. The menu is dead simple: choose your seafood and the sides and sauces are included. (off JI Pantai Jimbaran; meals 80,000-200,000Rp; ☉noon-10pm)

Drinking

Rock Bar
BAR

8 ♟ Map p62, A5

Star of a thousand glossy articles about Bali, this bar, perched 14m above the crashing Indian Ocean waves, is very popular. In fact at sunset the wait to ride the lift down to the bar can top one hour. Still, it's a dramatic location and late at night you can take in the stars without the crowds. (✆0361-702222; JI Karang Mas Sejahtera, Ayana Resort; ☉4pm-1am; 🛜)

Shopping

Jenggala Keramik Bali Ceramics
CERAMICS

9 🔒 Map p62, C5

This modern warehouse showcases beautiful ceramic homewares that are a favourite Balinese purchase. There's a viewing area where you can watch production, as well as a cafe. Ceramic courses are available for adults and children. (✆0361-703311; www.jenggala.com; JI Ulu Watu II; ☉8am-8pm)

Understand

Seafood in Jimbaran

From Jimabaran's beautiful beach you'll see a constant stream of fishing boats coming and going from the bustle and scrum of the Jimbaran Fish Market (p63), where Bali's restaurants purchase the fish caught in the local waters.

Pascal Chevillot, owner of Kerobokan's award-winning Sardine seafood restaurant, is there many mornings. 'New seafood arrives constantly as boats pull up to the beach. You know you'll find certain things like excellent shellfish all the time, but it's also an adventure as what's caught changes daily.'

Among the warren of shouting vendors, slippery, slimy footing and box-carrying porters elbowing past, Chevillot looks for the fish he considers Bali's best: 'Sea bream, mahi-mahi, skate and snapper are excellent but for me the greatest fun is the unexpected. Sometimes you see a fish they've caught that nobody can identify.'

Visiting the Market

Tourists can wander through the market throughout the day but Chevillot's advice is simple: 'Get there as early as possible and then stay out of the way. Wander around the dark interior and be ready to be constantly surprised.'

Although this is very much a working fish market, the vendors actually are happy to see visitors, figuring they will eat more seafood.

When a new boat pulls up to the beach, follow the excited crowd to see what bounty has appeared.

Enjoying Jimbaran's Seafood

Jimbaran's seafood warungs draw visitors from across the south. There are three distinct groups of seafood warungs spread out along the long beach. They do fresh barbecued seafood every evening (and noon at many). The open-sided affairs are right by the beach and perfect for enjoying sea breezes and sunsets. Tables and chairs are set up on the sand almost to the water's edge.

At the best places, the fish is soaked in a garlic and lime marinade, then doused with chilli and oil while it's grilling over coconut husks. Roaming bands perform songs along the lines of 'I've Gotta Be Me'.

Explore

Ulu Watu & Around

The surf breaks grouped along the west coast of the Bukit Peninsula are the stuff of legend, and draw board riders from across the world. Most visitors, however, are mere surfing poseurs and come for the idyllic little beaches at the base of the cliffs. And no visit is complete without a visit to Ulu Watu's monkey-filled temple.

The Region in a Day

☀ Rise early in hope of scoring a few waves to yourself at **Ulu Watu** (p72) while other surfers are still sleeping off the night before.

☀ Paddle in for an afternoon of exploring the many nooks and crannies of the Bukit Peninsula. Little beaches such as **Balangan** (p72), **Bingin** (p73) and **Padang Padang** (p72) are great finds that are worth minor treks across bad roads and along steep cliffside trails and stairs. Settle back on a lounger, enjoy a cold drink from a simple cafe and watch surfers pull into barrels offshore.

☾ Little places to stay – from simple surfer dives to posh boutique hotels – are where non-day-trippers vanish to after dark (nightlife is very limited). But everyone should make time for **Pura Luhur Ulu Watu** (p71) near sunset. The temple and its views are great and the **dance performance** (p75) is a must.

◉ Top Experiences

Hanging Out at Ulu Watu's Beaches (p68)

♥ Best of Bali

Surf Breaks
Ulu Watu (p72)

Balangan (p72)

Bingin (p73)

Impossibles (p73)

Beaches
Balangan Beach (p69)

Padang Padang Beach (p69)

For Kids
Pura Luhur Ulu Watu (p71)

Food
Om Burger (p75)

❶ Getting There & Around

🚗 **Taxi** Taxis from the Kuta–Seminyak area to the various beaches along the Bukit Peninsula and Ulu Watu will cost 125,000Rp to 200,000Rp one way. If day-tripping, be sure to arrange for a return as taxis don't hang around. Ulu Watu temple is often on tour itineraries.

Walk The various beaches are isolated from each other, so getting from one to the next requires some effort.

Top Experiences
Hanging Out at Ulu Watu's Beaches

One of Bali's hotspots is the booming west coast of the Bukit Peninsula with its string-of-pearls beaches. Often hidden at the base of cliffs, these white-sand visions of sunny pleasure are some of the best on Bali. You may have to drive along a road that barely qualifies as such and clamber down a steep path, but the reward is always worth it. Lazing away an afternoon at one of these coves is an essential Bali experience.

Balangan Beach

Don't Miss

Balangan Beach

Balangan Beach is a real find. A long and low strand at the base of the cliffs is covered with palm trees and fronted by a ribbon of near-white sand, picturesquely dotted with white sun umbrellas. Surfer bars (some with bare-bones sleeping rooms), cafes in shacks and even slightly more permanent guesthouses precariously line the shore where buffed First World bods soak up rays amid Third World sanitation. Balangan Beach is 6.5km off the main Ulu Watu road via Cenggiling.

Bingin Beach

An ever-evolving scene, Bingin comprises several unconventionally stylish lodgings scattered across – and down – the cliffs and on the strip of white sand below. A 1km lane turns off the paved road (look for the thicket of accommodation signs), which in turn branches off the main Ulu Watu road at the small village of Pecatu. After you pay an elderly resident for access, you get to the beach from a main parking area. Follow the steep steps and trail down.

Padang Padang Beach

Small in size but not in perfection (or popularity), this little cove is near the main Ulu Watu road where a stream flows into the sea. Parking is easy and it is a short walk through a temple and down a well-paved trail. If you're feeling adventurous, a much-longer stretch of white sand begins on the west side of the river. Ask locals how to get there.

☑ Top Tips

▶ Most of the beaches have namesake surf breaks offshore. Non-surfers enjoy watching the action on the water.

▶ Low-key cafes and vendors can be found on every beach.

▶ Although lacking sand, the cliffs at the Ulu Watu surf break have cafes with terraces, sun loungers and killer views.

▶ If you don't have your own transport (this is prime motorbike territory), arrange with your taxi or driver for pick-up at the end of the day.

✖ Take A Break

Rickety bamboo supports a lounging/drinking area at **Nasa Café** (meals from 30,000Rp; ⏱8am-11pm), where the view through the tufted palm leaves is of impossibly blue water streaked with white surf. Simple food, simple rooms and simple fun rule here and at similar joints on this tiny strip.

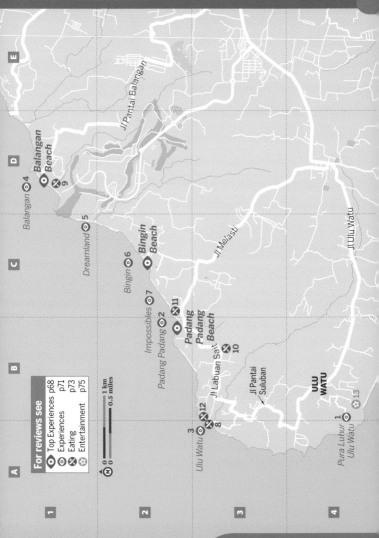

Balangan **Balangan Beach** ⊙4 ✕9

Dreamland ⊙5

Bingin **Bingin Beach** ⊙6 ⊙7

Impossibles ⊙7

Padang Padang ⊙2 ✕11 ⊙ **Padang Padang Beach** ✕10

Jl Pantai Balangan

Jl Melasti

Jl Ulu Watu

Jl Labuan Sait

Jl Pantai Suluban

ULU WATU ⊙13

⊙12 ✕8 ⊙3 Ulu Watu

Pura Luhur ⊙1 Ulu Watu ✪13

For reviews see
⊙ Top Experiences p68
⊙ Experiences   p71
✕ Eating   p73
✪ Entertainment   p75

0   1 km
0   0.5 miles

N

Pura Luhur Ulu Watu

Experiences

Pura Luhur Ulu Watu

HINDU TEMPLE

1 ◉ Map p70, B4

This important temple is perched precipitously on the southwestern tip of the peninsula, atop sheer cliffs that drop straight into the ceaseless surf. You enter through an unusual arched gateway flanked by statues of Ganesha. Inside, the walls of coral bricks are covered with intricate carvings of Bali's mythological menagerie. Only Hindu worshippers can enter the small inner temple that is built onto the jutting tip of land. However, the views of the endless swells of the Indian Ocean from the cliffs are almost spiritual. At sunset, walk around the clifftop to the left (south) of the temple to lose some of the crowd. (Jl Ulu Watu; admission incl sarong & sash rental adult/child 20,000/10,000Rp; ⊙8am-7pm)

☑ Top Tip

Damn Monkeys

Pura Luhur Ulu Watu is home to scores of grey monkeys. They're greedy little buggers: when they're not energetically fornicating they snatch sunglasses, handbags, hats and anything else within reach. Of course if you want to start a riot, show them your banana...

Padang Padang SURFING

2 ◉ Map p70, B2

Just 'Padang' for short, this super-shallow, left-hand reef break is offshore from the beach. If you can't surf tubes, backhand or forehand, don't go out: Padang is a tube. Many have compared it to a washing machine: it's not a spot for the faint-hearted. In August, international surfing competitions are held here; the nearby bridge is a top spot for viewing the action year-round.

Ulu Watu SURFING

3 ◉ Map p70, A3

When the surf at Kuta Beach is 5ft to 6ft, Ulu Watu, the most famous surfing break in Bali, will be 6ft to 8ft with bigger sets. It is 1km north of Pura Luhur Ulu Watu; look for the packs of scooters equipped with surfboard racks running down either of two roads that access parking areas and the flock of cafes and surf shops that line the cliffs overlooking the breaks.

Balangan SURFING

4 ◉ Map p70, D1

Off the long strip of sand that is Balangan Beach, the namesake surf break is a fast left over a shallow reef, unsurfable at low tide and good at midtide with anything over a 4ft swell; with an 8ft swell, this can be one of the classic waves.

Dreamland SURFING

5 ◉ Map p70, C1

You have to go through the sprawling, soul-destroying Pecatu Indah development to reach this break, but the waves are still here. At low 5ft swell, this solid peak offers a short, sharp right and a longer more tubular left.

Understand
Surfing the Bukit

With so many surf breaks – and surfers – along the west coast of the Bukit Peninsula, it's essential to know a little bit in advance. Observe where other surfers paddle out and follow them. If you are in doubt, ask someone. This can be especially true at Ulu Watu, where just getting in and out of the water through the cave at the base of the cliff can be a huge challenge.

Also understand that the breaks can get very crowded, especially on weekends and days when conditions are ideal. Here's how to fit in with the locals according to a local surfer. First, be polite! The local guys are usually cool but will stick up for each other if a tourist tries to steal a wave. If there are 50 surfers at a popular spot going for the same wave, let the locals have it and go down the beach a bit to where it's less crowded: you have a lot of choices.

Bingin

SURFING

6 ⊙ Map p70, C2

Given the walk down to Bingin Beach from the isolated parking area, you could be forgiven if you decide to leave your board up top, but don't. Waves here are best at midtide with a 6ft swell, when short but perfect left-hand barrels are formed, and you'll do well to have somebody on shore recording your action.

Impossibles

SURFING

7 ⊙ Map p70, C2

This outside reef break has three shifting peaks with fast left-hand tube sections that can join up if the conditions are perfect (low tide, 5ft swell), but don't stay on for too long, or you'll run out of water. It can be reached with a long paddle from either Bingin Beach or Padang Padang Beach.

Eating

Delpi Rock Lounge

CAFE $

8 ✖ Map p70, A3

At this branch of the Delpi empire you can nab a sunbed on a spectacular platform atop a rock nearly surrounded by surf. Further up the cliff there's a cafe that has three simple rooms for rent (from 350,000Rp). (meals from 50,000Rp; ☺noon-9pm)

> ### Understand
> ## Ulu Watu's Significance
>
> Ulu Watu is one of several important temples to the spirits of the sea along the south coast of Bali. In the 11th century the Javanese priest Empu Kuturan first established a temple here. The complex was added to by Nirartha, another Javanese priest who is known for the seafront temples at Tanah Lot, Rambut Siwi and Pura Sakenan. Nirartha retreated to Ulu Watu for his final days when he attained *moksa* (freedom from earthly desires).

Man Sis Cafe

CAFE $

9 ✖ Map p70, D1

A bamboo place on the sand that could star in any post-apocalyptic beach fantasy, Man Sis has a sign on a broken surfboard, grandma slicing vegetables up front, US$10 beds upstairs and cold Bintang around the clock. (☎0819 1653 8049; meals from 30,000Rp; ☺24hr)

Yeye's Warung

CAFE $

10 ✖ Map p70, B3

A gathering point away from the cliffs at a spot between Padang Padang and Ulu Watu, Yeye's has an easygoing ambience, cheapish beers, tasty Thai food and yes. good pizza. (Jl Labuan Sait; meals from 30,000Rp; ☺noon-midnight)

Understand

Bali's History

There are few traces of Stone Age people in Bali, although it's certain that the island was populated very early in prehistoric times. By the 9th century Bali had a society based on growing rice with the help of a complex irrigation system, probably very like that employed now; the Balinese had also begun to develop their rich cultural and artistic traditions.

Hinduism followed hot on the heels of wider cultural development, and as Islam swept through neighbouring Java in the following centuries, the kings and courtiers of the embattled Hindu Majapahit kingdom began crossing the straits into Bali, making their final exodus in 1478. The priest Nirartha brought many of the complexities of the Balinese Hindu religion to the island.

Europeans Arrive

The first Europeans to set foot in Bali itself were Dutch seamen in 1597. At that time, Balinese prosperity and artistic activity, at least among the royalty, was at a peak. By the 18th century, bickering among various Balinese princes caused the island's power structure to fragment. In 1846 the Dutch landed military forces in northern Bali. Focus turned to the south and in 1906 Dutch warships appeared at Sanur.

The Dutch forces landed despite Balinese opposition and had complete control of the island by 1908. Many thousands of Balinese – including royalty and priests – chose suicide in battle rather than occupation. Although under Dutch control and part of the Dutch East Indies, there was little development in Bali, and the common people noticed little difference between Dutch and royal rule.

Freedom

The Japanese occupied Bali in 1942 and conditions during WWII were grim. In August 1945, just days after the Japanese surrender, Sukarno, a prominent nationalist, proclaimed Indonesia's independence. Battles raged in Bali and elsewhere until the Dutch gave up and recognised Indonesia's independence in 1949. A prominent freedom fighter was Gusti Ngurah Rai, namesake of Bali's airport.

The tourism boom, which started in the early 1970s, has brought enormous changes for better and worse. However, Bali's unique culture has proved to be remarkably resilient even as visitor numbers top three million per year.

Understand
Religious Etiquette

- - - - - - - - - - - - - - - - - - - -

Just because the monkeys are misbehaving at Ulu Watu doesn't mean you can. The following are basic rules for visiting temples across Bali.

▶ If visiting a temple, cover shoulders and knees. A *selandong* (traditional scarf) or sash plus a sarong is usually provided for a small donation or as part of the admission fee.

▶ Women are asked not to enter temples if they're menstruating, pregnant or have recently given birth. At these times women are thought to be *sebel* (ritually unclean).

▶ Don't put yourself higher than a priest, particularly at festivals.

Om Burger
BURGERS $$

11 ⊗ Map p70, C2

'Superfood burgers' – that's the come-on at this joint with nice 2nd-floor views. The burgers are indeed super and are actually super-sized. There are intimations of health across the menu: baked sweet potato fries, vitamin-filled juices and more. It's very popular; expect to wait for a table at night. (☎0812 391 3617; Jl Labuan Sait; mains from 50,000Rp; ⊙8am-10pm; 🛜)

Single Fin
CAFE $$

12 ⊗ Map p70, B3

The views of the surf action from this triple-level cafe are breathtaking. Watch the neverending swells march in across the Indian from this cliffside perch and as the waves form, try to guess which

of the myriad surfers will catch a ride. Drinks here aren't cheap and the food is merely passable, but – especially at sunset – who cares? (☎0361-769941; meals from 60,000Rp; ⊙8am-11pm)

Entertainment

Kecak Dance
DANCE

13 ⭐ Map p70, B4

Although the performance obviously caters for tourists, the gorgeous setting at Pura Luhur Ulu Watu in a small amphitheatre in a leafy part of the grounds makes it one of the more evocative on the island. The views out to sea are as inspiring as the dance. It's very popular in high season. (Pura Luhur Ulu Watu, off Jl Ulu Watu; admission 100,000Rp; ⊙sunset)

Explore

Nusa Dua & Tanjung Benoa

Popular with holidaymakers who love large resorts, Nusa Dua seems far removed from Bali. In fact its huge beachside hotels and their hundreds of rooms could be anywhere in the world. It's a gated enclave where weeds – like uninvited locals – are marked for removal. Just to the north, slightly tatty Tanjung Benoa has a beach resort vibe without the artificial gloss.

The Region in a Day

Mornings are active: start with a market visit as part of the **Bumbu Bali Cooking School** (p79). Get wet and silly at one of Tanjung Benoa's many water-sports centres, such as **Benoa Marine Recreation** (p80). Straddle a banana boat and let the good times flow.

Relax into the afternoon with a languid stroll on the **beach promenade** (p80) or seek out the placid waters south of **Gegar Beach** (p80). Peruse beautiful Balinese art in the shady **Pasifika Museum** (p79) or lose yourself at a spa; every resort has an upscale one and you can enjoy the lauded touch of the local edition of Seminyak's **Jari Menari** (p80).

At night, consider skipping the many resort restaurants in favour of dining on the fabulous Balinese fare at **Bumbu Bali** (p81). Afterwards you might return to the beach promenade for a moonlit stroll with the heavenly light twinkling on the calm inshore waters.

♥ Best of Bali

Pampering
Jari Menari (p80)

Eating
Bumbu Bali (p81)

Bali for Kids
Benoa Marine Recreation (p80)

Art
Pasifika Museum (p79)

❶ Getting There & Around

🚗 **Taxi** Taxis from the airport will cost 100,000Rp to 150,000Rp. Metered taxis to/from Seminyak will cost about 90,000Rp. Note that the main road to the rest of Bali can get bogged down in traffic.

Walk A fine beach promenade runs much of the length of Nusa Dua and Tanjung Benoa. Otherwise, wide sidewalks abound in the former while the latter offers pedestrian peril along Jl Pratama.

1

Benoa Marine Recreation

7

Jl Pratama

For reviews see

| ⊙ | Experiences | p79 |
| ⊗ | Eating | p80 |

Ⓝ 0 ————————— 1 km
0 ————————— 0.5 miles

10 ⊗

Teluk Benoa

2

3 Bumbu Bali Cooking School

Jari Menari 6

Jl Pratama

Jl Ngurah Rai Bypass

Sri Lanka Beach

Selat Badung

3

Jl Pratama Raya

Jl Pratama Jln

4 Beach Promenade

NUSA DUA

Pasifika Museum 1

Jl Raya Bvalu Ungasan

BUALU

Golf Course

Jl Srikandi 9

4

Pantai Mengiat

Jl Terompong

Golf Course

5

5 Gegar Beach

8 ⊗

Jl Pura Gegar

Pura Gegar 2

KERRIE KERR/GETTY IMAGES ©

Seaweed farmer

Experiences

Pasifika Museum   MUSEUM

1 ◉ Map p78, C4

When groups from the nearby resorts aren't around, you'll probably have this large museum to yourself. Art of Pacific Ocean cultures spans several centuries and includes more than 600 paintings (don't miss the tikis). The influential wave of European artists who thrived in Bali in the early 20th century is well represented. Look for works by Arie Smit, Adrien Jean Le Mayeur de Merpres and Theo Meier. (📞0361-774559; Bali Collection Shopping Centre, Block P; admission 70,000Rp; ⊙10am-6pm)

Pura Gegar   HINDU TEMPLE

2 ◉ Map p78, B5

Just south of Gegar Beach is a bluff with a good cafe and a path that leads up to Pura Gegar, a compact temple shaded by gnarled old trees. Views are great and you can spot swimmers who've come south in the shallow, placid waters around the bluff for a little frolic.

Bumbu Bali Cooking School   COOKING

3 ◉ Map p78, B2

This much-lauded cooking school at the eponymous restaurant strives to get to the roots of Balinese cooking. Courses start with a 6am visit to Jimbaran's fish and morning markets, continues in the large kitchen and finishes with lunch. (☎0361-774502; www.balifoods.com; Jl Pratama; courses US$90; ⏰6am-3pm Mon, Wed & Fri)

Beach Promenade   WALKING

4 ◉ Map p78, C3

One of the nicest features of Nusa Dua is the 5km-long beach promenade that stretches the length of the resort and continues north along much of the beach in Tanjung Benoa.

Gegar Beach   BEACH

5 ◉ Map p78, B5

The once gem-like Gegar Beach is now gem-sized with the addition of a 700-room Mulia resort. The public area has some cafes, rental loungers and water activities (kayak rental 30,000Rp per hour); it gets jammed on weekends. Boats out to the Nusa Dua Surf Break

---

Q Local Life
Benoa's Places of Worship

The village of **Benoa** is a fascinating little fishing settlement that makes for a good stroll. Amble the narrow lanes of the peninsula's tip for a multicultural feast. Within 100m of each other are a brightly coloured **Chinese Buddhist temple**, a domed **mosque** and a **Hindu temple** with a nicely carved triple entrance. Enjoy views of the busy channel to the port.

---

beyond the reef costs 150,000Rp. You can still use the immaculate public sands in front of the resorts. (admission 5000Rp)

Jari Menari   SPA

6 ◉ Map p78, B2

This branch of the famed Seminyak original offers all the same exquisite massages by the expert all-male staff. Call for transport. (☎0361-778084; www.jarimenarinusadua.com; Jl Pratama; massages from 350,000Rp; ⏰9am-9pm)

Benoa Marine Recreation   WATER SPORTS

7 ◉ Map p78, B1

One of many water-sports centres along the beach in Tanjung Benoa, BMR has a slightly more slick operation than the others but all rumble in the mornings as the buses pull in with day-tripping groups. Note that virtually all the prices for activities are highly negotiable. (☎0361-771757; www.bmrbali.com; Jl Pratama; ⏰8am-4pm)

Eating

Nusa Dua Beach Grill   INTERNATIONAL $

8 🍴 Map p78, B5

A hidden gem, this warm-hued cafe is south of Gegar Beach and the huge Mulia resort on foot, but a circuitous 1.5km by car via the temple. The drinks menu is long, the seafood fresh and the atmosphere heavy with assignations. Lounge your afternoon away in the laid-back bar. Call for local transport. (0361-743 4779; Jl Pura Gegar; meals 50,000-150,000Rp; 8am-10pm)

Warung Dobiel
BALINESE $

9 ✗ Map p78, B4

A bit of authentic food action amid the bland streets of Nusa, this is a good stop for *babi guling*. Pork soup is the perfect taste-bud awakener, while the jackfruit is redolent with spices. Diners perch on stools and share tables; service can be slow and tours may mob the place. Watch out for 'foreigner' pricing. (Jl Srikandi; meals from 25,000Rp; 10am-3pm)

Bumbu Bali
BALINESE $$

Long-time resident and cookbook author Heinz von Holzen (see 3 Map p78, B2), his wife Puji and a well-trained and enthusiastic staff serve exquisitely flavoured dishes at this superb restaurant. Many diners opt for one of several lavish set menus.

The *rijstaffel* (a selection of dishes served with rice) shows the range of cooking in the kitchen, from satays served on their own little coconut husk grill to the tender *be celeng base manis* (pork in sweet soy sauce), with a dozen

☑ Top Tip
Spa Happy
Virtually every resort in Nusa Dua and Tanjung Benoa has an in-house spa. Many are quite large – as you'd expect at properties with hundreds of rooms – and each year, the overall standard becomes more lavish. If you're staying at one of the big hotels, you may not ever need to leave the property for a spa – or leave the spa for that matter.

more courses in between. (0361-774502; www.balifoods.com; Jl Pratama; mains from 90,000Rp, set menus from 270,000Rp; noon-9pm)

Bali Cardamon
ASIAN $$

10 ✗ Map p78, B1

A cut above most of the other restaurants on the Jl Pratama strip, this ambitious spot has a creative kitchen that takes influences from across Asia. It has some excellent dishes, including pork belly seasoned with star anise. Sit under the frangipani trees or in the dining room. (0361-773745; www.balicardamon.com; Jl Pratama 97; mains from 60,000Rp; 8am-10pm)

Explore

Sanur

The first Western artists to settle in Bali did so around Sanur more than 100 years ago. It's easy to see why: there's a long family-friendly beach protected by reefs, plenty of shady palm trees overhead and cool breezes off the ocean. Sanur isn't a party town, so visitors looking for serenity will be suitably chilled out here.

The Region in a Day

☼ Take advantage of the eastern light to hit **Sanur Beach** (p86) in the morning. Watch people fishing in traditional ways and try some water fun with **Surya Water Sports** (p86). Or get serious and get your scuba certification at **Crystal Divers** (p86).

☼ Enjoy a leisurely lunch with views over the water to Nusa Lembongan and Nusa Penida. **Warung Pantai Indah** (p88) and **Warung Mak Beng** (p87) are locally flavoured options. Once past noon, the shadows of the palm trees lengthen on the beach, so it's a good time for some spa action at **Jamu Traditional Spa** (p85) or **Glo Day Spa** (p87). Or just hit the shops. Jl Tamblingan has many choices including **A-Krea** (p89) for Bali-designed goods and **Ganesha Bookshop** (p89) for a perfect poolside read.

☾ For dinner, Jl Tamblingan again offers many choices. Try something Indonesian at **Pregina Warung** (p89) or go with Asian flair at **Three Monkeys Cafe** (p89). At the latter you can hear live jazz some nights. Finish off your evening with a stroll on the **Beachfront Walk** (p85), which ideally will offer moonlit views over the water.

 Best of Bali

Diving & Snorkelling
Crystal Divers (p86)

Surya Water Sports (p86)

Beaches
Sanur Beach (p86)

Pampering
Jamu Traditional Spa (p85)

Power of Now Oasis (p87)

Bali for Kids
Sanur Beach (p86)

Surya Water Sports (p86)

Bali Kite Festival (p89)

Art
Museum Le Mayeur (p85)

➊ Getting There & Around

🚗 **Taxi** Taxis from the airport will cost about 110,000Rp. A cab to/from Seminyak will cost about 70,000Rp and take from 20 minutes to an hour depending on traffic.

Walk You can easily walk the length of Sanur on the lovely beachfront walk. The main spine, Jl Tamblingan, is easily walkable.

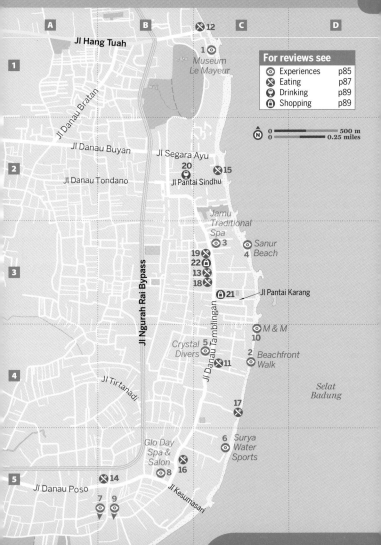

JI Hang Tuah

A   B   C   D

❌ 12

1 ◉
Museum
Le Mayeur

JI Danau Bratan

For reviews see

◉ Experiences   p85
❌ Eating   p87
🍷 Drinking   p89
🛍 Shopping   p89

JI Danau Buyan

JI Segara Ayu

⬆N 0 ▬▬▬▬▬ 500 m
    0 ▬▬▬▬▬ 0.25 miles

JI Danau Tondano

20 🍷
JI Pantai Sindhu   ❌ 15

Jamu
Traditional
Spa

◉ 3   ◉ Sanur
       4 Beach

19 ❌
22 🛍
13 ❌
18 ❌

🛍 21   JI Pantai Karang

JI Ngurah Rai Bypass

JI Danau Tambingan

◉ M & M
10

Crystal 5
Divers ◉   2 ◉ Beachfront
❌ 11   Walk

JI Tirtanadi

Selat
Badung

17
❌

Glo Day
Spa &
Salon   6 ◉ Surya
❌ 16   Water
◉ 8   Sports

❌ 14
JI Danau Poso

JI Kesumasari

7   9
◉   ◉

Gardens of Museum Le Mayeur

Experiences

Museum Le Mayeur MUSEUM

1 ⊙ Map p84, C1

Le Mayeur de Merpres (1880–1958) arrived in Bali in 1932. Three years later, he met and married the beautiful Legong dancer Ni Polok when she was just 15. They lived in this compound, which houses the museum, when Sanur was still a quiet fishing village. After the artist's death, Ni Polok lived in the house until she died in 1985. (☏0361-286201; adult/child 10,000/5000Rp; ⊗8am-4pm Sat-Thu, to 12.30pm Fri)

Beachfront Walk WATERFRONT

2 ⊙ Map p84, C4

Sanur's beachfront walk was the first in Bali and has been delighting locals and visitors alike from day one. Over 4km long, it curves past resorts, beachfront cafes, wooden fishing boats under repair and quite a few elegant old villas built decades ago by the wealthy expats who fell under Bali's spell. While you stroll, look out across the water to Nusa Penida.

Jamu Traditional Spa SPA

3 ⊙ Map p84, C3

The beautifully carved teak and stone entry sets the mood at this gracious spa, which offers a range of treatments including a popular Earth & Flower

Understand
Sanur's Rulers & Artists

Sanur was one of the places favoured by Westerners during the pre-WWII discovery of Bali. Artists Miguel Covarrubias, Adrien Jean Le Mayeur de Merpres and Walter Spies, anthropologist Jane Belo and choreographer Katharane Mershon spent time here. The first tourist bungalows appeared in Sanur in the 1940s and '50s, and retiring expats followed. During this period Sanur was ruled by insightful priests and scholars, who recognised both the opportunities and the threats presented by expanding tourism. Horrified at the high-rise Grand Bali Beach Hotel, they imposed the famous rule that no building could be higher than a coconut palm. They also established village cooperatives that owned land and ran tourist businesses, ensuring that economic benefits remained in the community. Their influence remains strong, and Sanur is one of the few communities still ruled by members of the Brahmana caste and is known as a home of sorcerers and healers. The black-and-white chequered cloth known as *kain poleng*, which symbolises the balance of good and evil, is emblematic of Sanur.

Body Mask and a Kemiri Nut Scrub. (☑0361-286595; www.jamutraditionalspa.com; Jl Danau Tamblingan 41, Tandjung Sari Hotel; massages from 600,000Rp; ⊗8am-9pm)

Sanur Beach
BEACH

4 ◎ Map p84, C3

Sanur Beach curves in a southwesterly direction and stretches for over 5km. It is mostly clean and overall quite serene – much like the town itself. Offshore reefs mean that the surf is reduced to tiny waves lapping the shore. With a couple of unfortunate exceptions, the resorts along the sand are low-key, leaving the beach uncrowded.

Crystal Divers
DIVING

5 ◎ Map p84, C4

This slick diving operation has its own hotel (the Santai) and a large diving pool. Recommended for beginners, the shop offers a long list of courses, including PADI open-water courses for US$500. (☑0361-286737; www.crystal-divers.com; Jl Danau Tamblingan 168; intro dives from US$80)

Surya Water Sports
WATER SPORTS

6 ◎ Map p84, C5

One of several water-sports operations along the beach, Surya is the largest. You can go parasailing (US$20 per ride), snorkelling by boat (US$40, two hours) or rent a kayak and paddle the smooth waters (US$10 per hour). (☑0361-287956; Jl Duyung 10; ⊗9am-5pm; 🚸)

Power of Now Oasis

YOGA

7 Map p84, B5

Enjoy a yoga class in this lovely bamboo pavilion on Sanur Beach. Several levels are offered. (☑0813 3831 5032; www.powerofnowoasis.com; Beachfront Walk, Hotel Mercure; classes from 80,000Rp; ⊙varies)

Glo Day Spa & Salon

SPA

8 Map p84, B5

An insider pick by the many local Sanur expats, Glo eschews a fancy setting for a clean-lined storefront. Services and treatments run the gamut, from skin and nail care to massages and spa therapies. (☑0361-282826; www.glo-day-spa.com; Jl Danau Poso 57, Gopa Town Centre; sessions from 195,000Rp; ⊙8am-6pm)

Rip Curl School of Surf

WINDSURFING

9 Map p84, B5

Sanur's reef-protected waters and regular offshore breezes make for good windsurfing. (☑0361-287749; www.ripcurlschoolofsurf.com; Beachfront Walk, Sanur Beach Hotel; lessons from 1,100,000Rp, rental per hr from 100,000Rp; ⊙8am-5pm)

M & M

KITESURFING

10 Map p84, C4

Made Sambuk offers kitesurfing lessons right on the beach. (☑0813 3745 2825; Beachfront Walk; lessons from US$90, rental per 90min 350,000Rp; ⊙9am-6pm)

Eating

Manik Organik

ORGANIC $

11 Map p84, C4

Actual trees shade the serene terrace at this creative and healthful cafe. Vegetarians are well cared for, but there are also meaty dishes made with free-range chicken and the like. Smoothies include the fortifying 'immune tonic'. (www.manikorganikbali.com; Jl Danau Tamblingan 85; meals from 50,000Rp; ⊙8am-10pm; ☑)

Warung Mak Beng

BALINESE $

12 Map p84, C1

You don't need a menu at this local favourite: all you can order is its legendary BBQ fish, which comes with various sides and some tasty soup. Service is quick, the air fragrant and diners of all stripes very happy. (☑0361-282633; Jl Hang Tuah 45; meals 35,000Rp; ⊙11am-9pm)

☑ Top Tip

Bali's Oldest Artefact?

A stone pillar, down a narrow lane to the left as you face Pura Belangjong, is Bali's oldest dated artefact and has inscriptions recounting military victories of more than a thousand years ago. The inscriptions are in Sanskrit and are evidence of Hindu influence 300 years before the arrival of the Majapahit court. This is a good excuse for a non-beach walk followed by a meal at Sari Bundo.

Porch Cafe
CAFE $

13 🍴 Map p84, C3

Housed in a traditional wooden building, this cafe offers a mix of comfort food, including burgers, and freshly baked goods, such as ciabatta. Sit at a table on the porch or shut it all out in the air-con inside. Popular for breakfast, there's a long list of fresh juices. Flashbacks, a cute guesthouse, is in the rear. (📞0361-281682; Jl Danau Tamblingan, Flashbacks; meals from 40,000Rp; ⏱7am-10pm; ❄🛜)

Sari Bundo
INDONESIAN $

14 🍴 Map p84, B5

This spotless Padang-style shopfront is one of several at the south end of Sanur. Choose from an array of fresh and spicy food. The curry chicken is a fiery treat that will have your tongue alternatively loving and hating you. (📞0361-281389; Jl Danau Poso; mains from 20,000Rp; ⏱24hr)

Minami
JAPANESE $$

15 🍴 Map p84, C2

With its minimalist white decor, open-air atmosphere and range of ultra-fresh fish, this authentic Japanese place is a great find on the beach. There's sushi plus various tempura, gyoza, salads, noodle dishes and more. Standards are very high. (📞0812 8613 4471; Beachfront Walk, Segara Village Hotel; mains from 50,000Rp; ⏱11am-11pm)

Char Ming
ASIAN $$

16 🍴 Map p84, B5

Barbecue with a French accent. A daily menu board lists the fresh seafood available; look for regional dishes, many with modern flair. The highly stylised location features lush plantings and carved-wood details from vintage Javanese and Balinese structures. (📞0361-288029; www.charming-bali.com; Jl Danau Tamblingan 97; meals 100,000-200,000Rp; ⏱6-11pm)

Warung Pantai Indah
CAFE $$

17 🍴 Map p84, C4

Sit at battered tables and chairs on the sand under a tin roof at this timeless beach cafe. Just north of the Hotel Peneeda View and near some of Sanur's most expensive private beach villas, this outpost of good cheer has cheap beer, regular specials on fresh-grilled seafood and splendid views. (Beachfront Walk; mains 40,000-100,000Rp; ⏱noon-11pm)

JONES/SHIMLOCK: SECRET SEA VISIONS/GETTY IMAGES ©

Bali Kite Festival

Three Monkeys Cafe
ASIAN $$

18 Map p84, C3

This branch of the splendid Ubud original is no mere knock-off. Spread over two floors, there's cool jazz playing in the background and live performances some nights. Set well back from the road, you can enjoy Sanur's best coffee drinks on sofas or chairs. The creative menu mixes Western fare with pan-Asian creations. (☑0361-286002; Jl Danau Tamblingan; meals 60,000-150,000Rp; ⊙8am-11pm; 🛜)

Pregina Warung
BALINESE $$

19 Map p84, C3

Classic Balinese duck dishes and crowd-pleasers such as satay are mainstays of the interesting menu at this restaurant that serves local foods several cuts above the all-too-common bland tourist versions. The dining room has spare, stylish wooden decor. (☑0361-283353; Jl Danau Tamblingan 106; mains 40,000-80,000Rp; ⊙11am-10pm)

Drinking

Kalimantan
BAR

20 🍷 Map p84, B2

This veteran boozer has an old South Pacific thatched charm and is one of many casual bars on this street. Enjoy cheap drinks under the palms in the large, shady garden. The Mexican food features homegrown chilli peppers. (Borneo Bob's; ☑0361-289291; Jl Pantai Sindhu 11; mains from 40,000Rp; ⊙11am-midnight)

🔍 Local Life
Sanur's Kites

You hear them overhead: huge kites 10m or more in length, with tails stretching another 100m and sporting noise-makers producing eerie humming and buzzing noises.

Each July hundreds of Balinese and international teams descend – as it were – on open spaces north of Sanur for the **Bali Kite Festival**. The action is centred on Padang Galak Beach, about 2km up the coast from Sanur. Peak time for catching the high-flying art over Sanur is May to September.

Shopping

A-Krea
CLOTHING

21 🔒 Map p84, C3

A range of items designed and made in Bali are available in this attractive store that takes the colours of the island and gives them a minimalist flair. Clothes, accessories, housewares and more are all handmade. (☑0361-286101; Jl Danau Tamblingan 51; ⊙9am-8pm)

Nogo
TEXTILES

22 🔒 Map p84, C3

Look for the wooden loom out front of this classy store, which bills itself as the 'Bali Ikat Centre.' The goods are gorgeous and easy to enjoy in the air-con comfort. (☑0361-288765; www.nogobali.com; Jl Danau Tamblingan 104; ⊙9am-8pm)

Top Experiences
Nusa Lembongan

Getting There

⚓ **Boat** Public boats
from Sanur at 8am
cost 60,000Rp one
way (1¾ to two hours).
Fast tourist boats
include those run by
Scoot (www.scoot
cruise.com) and cost
around US$60 return
including hotel pick-up.

Alluring when seen from Sanur and east Bali, Nusa Lembongan is one of three islands that together comprise the Nusa Penida archipelago. It's the Bali many imagine but never find: rooms right on the beach, cheap beers with incredible sunsets, days spent surfing and diving, and nights spent engrossed in a new book or hanging with new friends. You can savour this bliss in a day or two away from the bright lights of south Bali.

Nusa Lembongan

Don't Miss

Jungutbatu Beach

Jungutbatu beach, a lovely arc of white sand with clear blue water, has superb views across to Gunung Agung in Bali. The village itself is pleasant, with quiet lanes, no cars and a couple of temples.

Mushroom Bay

Gorgeous little Mushroom Bay, unofficially named for the mushroom corals offshore, is a perfect crescent of white-sand beach. The most pleasant way to get here from Jungutbatu is to walk along the trail that starts from the southern end of the main beach and follows the coastline for 1km or so past a couple of little beaches.

Diving & Snorkelling

There are great diving possibilities around the islands, from shallow and sheltered reefs to very demanding drift dives. Notable sites include **Blue Corner** and **Jackfish Point** off Nusa Lembongan. **World Diving** (✆0812 390 0686 ; www.world-diving.com; 2 dives from US$85, open-water course US$395), based at Pondok Baruna on Jungutbatu Beach, is well regarded and offers various courses. Good snorkelling can also be had just off the Mushroom Bay and Bounty **pontoons** off Jungutbatu Beach, as well as in areas off the north coast of the island.

Surfing

Surfing here is best in the dry season (April to September), when the winds come from the southeast. Take note, however, that it's not for beginners. There are three main breaks on the reef, all aptly named. From north to south they are **Shipwrecks**, **Lacerations** and **Playgrounds**.

☑ Top Tips

▸ There are lots of simple guesthouses and a few small upmarket hotels.

▸ You can charter a boat from 150,000Rp per hour for snorkelling and for getting out to some surf breaks.

▸ You can easily walk to most places; bicycles cost 30,000Rp per day.

▸ There's no reliable ATM.

▸ A walk around much of the island is an all-day adventure.

✕ Take a Break

There are numerous beach cafes with all the usual standards plus fabulous views. For a cut above, **Indiana Kenanga** (✆0828 9708 4367; www.indiana-kenanga-villas.com; Jungutbatu Beach; r US$150-600; ❋ 🖘 ☎) looks plucked from a glossy magazine and has an all-day menu of seafood, sandwiches and various surprises cooked up by a French chef.

Explore

Denpasar

Bali's capital, home to most of the island's people and covering much of south Bali, shouldn't be overlooked by visitors. Here, chaotic and confusing streets mix with wide parks and boulevards that have a certain grandeur. Denpasar also boasts the island's main museums and largest markets as well as a range of excellent restaurants.

The Sights in a Day

Visit the markets, **Pasar Badung** (p96) and **Pasar Kumbasari** (p96), in the morning when selection is greatest. The fruits and vegetables still look fresh and the flowers used for offerings are at their colourful best.

Lunch at any of many local eateries, such as **Café Teduh** (p96) and **Cak Asmo** (p96), which have excellent local dishes cooked to the standards demanded by the choosy Balinese. After, absorb Bali's history and culture at the comprehensive **Museum Negeri Propinsi Bali** (p95), the important temple **Pura Jagatnatha** (p95) and the surprisingly entertaining **Bajra Sandhi Monument** (p95).

For visitors, Denpasar is an easy day trip from across south Bali and Ubud. However, it offers few reasons to linger after late afternoon.

Best of Bali

Shopping
Pasar Badung (p96)

Adil (p96)

Art
Museum Negeri Propinsi Bali (p95)

Getting There & Around

Taxi Taxis from Sanur cost about 50,000Rp, from Seminyak about 70,000Rp. Expect heavy traffic.

Walk You can easily walk between the main markets and Museum Negeri Propinsi Bali. Most restaurants are located in Renon, a long walk from the markets or a 15,000Rp taxi ride.

KEDATON

RENON

SANGLAH

Jl Dewi Madri

Jl Cok Agung Tresna

Jl Kartawijaya

Bajra Sandhi Monument

Jl Drupadi

Jl Dr Kusumah Atmaja

Jl Badak Agung

Jl Panjaitan

Jl Raya Puputan

Jl Jayagiri

Letda Tantular

Tukad Gangga

Jl Ki Hajar Dewantara

Jl Kapten Agung

Sungai Badung

Jl Surapati

Pura Jagatnatha

Museum Negeri Propinsi Bali

Jl Sugianyar

Jl Sudirman

Jl Udayana

Jl Diponegoro

Jl Teuku Umar

Jl Gajah Mada

Jl Kartini

Jl Hasanudin

Jl Nusakambangan

Sungai Badung

Jl Thamrin

500 m
0.25 miles

TOM COCKREM/GETTY IMAGES ©

Full Moon festival, Pura Jagatnatha

Experiences

Museum Negeri Propinsi Bali

MUSEUM

1 ⊙ Map p94, B1

Think of this as the British Museum or Smithsonian of Balinese culture. It's all here, but you do have to work at sorting it out. The museum could use a dose of curatorial energy; most displays are labelled in English. Museum staff often play music on a bamboo gamelan to magical effect; visit in the afternoon when it's uncrowded. Ignore 'guides' who offer little except a chance to part with US$5 or US$10. (☎0361-222680; adult/child 10,000/5000Rp; ⊙8am-12.30pm Fri, to 4pm Sat-Thu)

Pura Jagatnatha

TEMPLE

2 ⊙ Map p94, B1

The state temple, built in 1953, is dedicated to the supreme god, Sanghyang Widi. Part of its significance is its statement of monotheism. Although the Balinese recognise many gods, the belief in one supreme god (who can have many manifestations) brings Balinese Hinduism into conformity with the first principle of Pancasila – the 'Belief in One God.' (Jl Surapati)

Bajra Sandhi Monument

MONUMENT

3 ⊙ Map p94, E4

This huge monument is as big as its name. Inside the vaguely Borobudur-like structure are dioramas tracing Bali's history. Taking the name as a cue, you won't be surprised that they have a certain jingoistic soap-opera quality. But they're a fun diversion. Note that in the portrayal of the 1906 battle with the Dutch, the King of Badung is literally a sitting target. (Monument to the Struggle of the People of Bali; ☎0361-264517; Jl Raya Puputan, Renon; adult/child 10,000/5000Rp; ☽9am-4.30pm)

Eating

Café Teduh   INDONESIAN $

4 ✕ Map p94, B3

Amid the big shopping malls, this little oasis is hidden down a tiny lane. Hanging orchids, trees, flowers and ponds with fountains are a good setting to enjoy food from Manado. Try *ayam dabu-dabu* (grilled chicken with chilli paste, tomatoes, shallots, lemongrass and spices, or *nasi bakar cumi hitam* (rice and marinated squid wrapped in banana leaf and grilled). (☎0361-221631; off Jl Diponegoro; mains 10,000-20,000Rp; ☽10am-10pm; ☎)

Cak Asmo   INDONESIAN, CHINESE $

6 ✕ Map p94, D4

Join the government workers and students from the nearby university for superb dishes cooked to order in the bustling kitchen. Order the buttery and crispy *cumi cumi* (calamari) with *telor asin* sauce (a heavenly mixture of eggs and garlic). Fruity ice drinks are a cool-

ing treat. An English-language menu makes ordering a breeze. (Jl Tukad Gangga; meals from 25,000Rp; ☽8am-10pm)

Shopping

Pasar Badung   MARKET

7 🔒 Map p94, A1

Bali's largest food market is busy in the morning and evening (although dull and sleepy from 2pm to 4pm); it's a great place to browse and bargain. You'll find produce and food from all over the island, as well as easy-to-assemble temple offerings that are popular with working women. (Jl Gajah Mada; ☽6am-8pm)

Adil   TEXTILES

8 🔒 Map p94, B1

Jammed into a string of fabric stores just east of Pasar Badung, this narrow shop stands out for its huge selection of genuine Balinese batik. The colours and patterns are bewildering, while the clearly marked reasonable prices are not. (☎0361-234601; Jl Sulawesi 13; ☽9am-6pm)

Pasar Kumbasari   MARKET

9 🔒 Map p94, A1

Handicrafts, a plethora of vibrant fabrics and costumes decorated with gold are just some of the goods at this huge market across the river from Pasar Badung. Note that the malls have taken their toll and there are a lot of empty stalls. (Jl Gajah Mada; ☽8am-6pm)

Understand

Bali's Dance & Music

- -

Bali's renowned dance, which is accompanied by its unique and lyrical gamelan music, is easily enjoyed, even during a short visit. For many it's a highlight of their trip and is what sets Bali apart from other destinations.

If you visit in June and July, be sure to check out the **Bali Arts Festival** (www.baliartsfestival.com; Taman Wedhi Budaya; ⊘mid-Jun–mid-Jul), a huge celebration of Balinese dance and music that takes place at venues in Denpasar.

Dance

Balinese love a blend of seriousness and slapstick, and this shows in their dances. Some have a decidedly comic element, with clowns who convey the story and also act as a counterpoint to the staid, noble characters. Balinese dance is precise, jerky and jumpy, remarkably like Balinese music. Every movement of wrist, hand and fingers is charged with meaning, while facial expressions are carefully choreographed to convey the character of the dance.

Probably the best known of the dances is the Kecak, which tells a tale from the *Ramayana,* one of the great Hindu holy books. Throughout performances the dancing and chanting are superbly synchronised with an eerily exciting coordination. Add in actors posing as an army of monkeys and you have an unbeatable spectacle.

Another popular dance for tourists shows a battle between good (the Barong) and bad (the Rangda). The Barong is a strange but good, mischievous and fun-loving shaggy dog-lion. The widow-witch Rangda is bad through and through.

The most graceful of Balinese dances, Legong, is performed by young girls. It is so important in Balinese culture that in old age a classic dancer will be remembered as a 'great Legong'.

You'll find exceptional dance performances in and around Ubud. Some south Bali hotels offer abbreviated performances with just a few musicians and a couple of dancers.

Music

Balinese music is based around an ensemble known as a gamelan, or *gong*. A full orchestra has up to 25 shiny bronze instruments. Although it sounds strange at first with its noisy, jangly percussion, it's exciting, enjoyable, melodic and at times haunting. Gamelan is a part of most dance performances.

Explore

Ubud

When you think about what really sets Bali apart from other beachy destinations, it is the culture, the rice fields and the inherent charm of the people – qualities that Ubud has in spades. Bali's rich artistic and dance traditions are here to enjoy. And there's plenty of sybaritic spas and splendid restaurants to keep things from getting too high-minded.

The Region in a Day

🌅 Get up with the sun and walk through Ubud's **rice fields** (p100). Afterwards try to think up new words for 'green' and 'beautiful' as you enjoy a coffee at one Ubud's many great cafes, such as **Anomali Coffee** (p109) or **Coffee Studio Seniman** (p110). Now might be a good time for some shopping at the boutiques on Jl Dewi Sita.

☀️ Have a healthy lunch at **Bali Buda** (p110), or go completely local at **Warung Ibu Oka** (p110). Now enjoy some pampering: consider yoga at **Yoga Barn** (p103), a range of therapies at **Taksu Spa** (p108) or a luxurious massage at **Bali Botanica Day Spa** (p108).

🌙 No night is complete without a taste of Ubud's famed dance culture. Choose your **dance performance** (p114) and enjoy traditions that are the very soul of the Balinese. After, savour dinner at **Locavore** (p113), **Mozaic** (p113) or **Pica** (p111). Ubud goes to bed early: after a glimpse of the moonlight on the rice fields, enjoy a great night's sleep in the cool mountain air; or extend your evening with some Western tunes at the **Jazz Café** (p113).

For a local's day in Ubud, see p102.

◎ Top Experiences
Touring Ubud's Rice Fields (p100)

◯ Local Life
A Perfect Ubud Day (p102)

♥ Best of Bali

Nightlife
Jazz Café (p113)
Room 4 Dessert (p110)

Eating
Locavore (p113)
Mozaic (p113)
Warung Pulau Kelapa (p109)
Pica (p111)
Alchemy (p112)

Shopping
Ganesha Bookshop (p116)
Threads of Life Indonesian Textile Arts Center (p116)

Bali for Kids
Sacred Monkey Forest Sanctuary (p106)

❶ Getting There & Around

🚗 **Car** A car and driver to/from Ubud and south Bali will cost about US$25. A metered taxi will run about 180,000Rp.

Walk Ubud is all about walking although local guys offer 'transport' for about 20,000Rp to 40,000Rp depending on distance.

Top Experiences
Touring Ubud's Rice Fields

There's nothing like a walk through the verdant rice fields of Ubud to make all right with the world. These unbelievably green and ancient terraces spill down lush hillsides to rushing rivers below. As you wander along, you can hear the symphony of frogs, bugs and the constant gurgle of water coursing through channels. Most fields produce three crops a year and even on a short walk you'll see tender shoots, vibrant seas of green and the grain-heavy heads of mature plants.

Rice fields, Ubud

Don't Miss

Walk It Yourself

From the Ibah Luxury Villas driveway in Campuan, take the path to the left, where a walkway crosses the river to the small and serene Pura Gunung Lebah. Follow the concrete path north onto the ridge between the two rivers where you can see the rice fields above Ubud folding over the hills in all directions.

Bali Bird Walks

For keen birdwatchers, this popular **tour** (📞0361-975009; www.balibirdwalk.com; tours US$37; 🕑9am-12.30pm Tue, Fri, Sat & Sun), started by Victor Mason, draws flocks. A gentle morning's walk will give you the opportunity to see maybe 30 of the 100 or so local species. The tours leave from the former Beggar's Bush Bar on Jl Raya Campuan.

Herb Walks

Enjoy a three-hour **walk** (📞0812 381 6024; www.bali herbalwalk.com; walks US$18; 🕑8.30am) through lush Bali landscape; medicinal and cooking herbs and plants are identified and explained in their natural environment. Includes herbal drinks.

Banyan Tree Cycling

These day-long **tours** (📞805 1620, 0813 3879 8516; www.banyantreebiketours.com; tours from 450,000Rp) of remote villages in the hills above Ubud are very popular and have inspired a bevy of competitors. It's locally owned, and the tours emphasise interaction with villagers.

Make a Discovery

Parts of Ubud may seem chock-a-block with development but you'd be surprised how often you can find beautifully emerald green rice fields, just by ducking down a lane. Try this along Jl Bisma or even Monkey Forest Rd.

☑ Top Tips

▶ Tail a family of local ducks through the rice fields; if a path peters out, you can always go back.

▶ Bring water, a good hat, decent shoes and wet-weather gear for the afternoon showers.

▶ Try to start walks at daybreak, before it gets too hot.

▶ Some entrepreneurial rice farmers have erected little toll gates across their fields. You can detour around them or pay a fee (never, ever accede to more than 10,000Rp).

✕ Take A Break

A stroll through Ubud's beautiful rice fields calls for a snack. Bali Buddha has an organic market and bakery, **BudaMart** (www.balibuda.com; Jl Raya Ubud; 🕑8am-8pm), where you can choose from a range of tasty treats to stash in your daypack (snacks from 10,000Rp). The blueberry muffins are especially good.

Local Life
A Perfect Ubud Day

Spas, shopping, cafes, markets, temples, dance and more can fill your Ubud days. Here's an ideal stroll combining a little of all that will work whether you are staying for a few days or are day-tripping. This walk takes you through the heart of the town, and you'll find plenty of discoveries along the way.

....

❶ Cleanse Yourself Inside & Out

There are so many places in Ubud for health and spa treatments that you almost need therapy to sort through them. But an excellent place to start is **Ubud Sari Health Resort** (☏0361-974393; www. ubudsari.com; Jl Kajeng; 1hr massages from US$15; ⊙9am-8pm), where function trumps form. The setting is pastoral and includes all manner of herbs and healing plants.

❷ Ubud's Water Temple

An oasis in the heart of Ubud, **Pura Taman Saraswati** (Jl Raya Ubud) is one of the town's most picturesque spots. Waters from the temple at the rear feed a pond overflowing with iconic lotus blossoms. There are usually a few wannabe artists trying to capture the moment. No matter how frenetic the traffic is outside, here you'll feel nothing but calm.

❸ Ubud's Hidden Produce Market

Hidden within the overcrowded and euphemistically named art market is this real, working **Produce Market** (Jl Raya Ubud; ⏲6am-1pm). Get here early enough and you'll find Ubud's top chefs bargaining for their day's ingredients. Browse Bali's fab range of fresh foodstuffs and see how many types of fruit you *can't* identify.

❹ Dewi Sita Creations

The relatively short, curving and hilly Jl Dewi Sita is lined with some of Ubud's most creative shops. Everything from handmade paper to jewellery to luscious beauty products can be found at its little boutiques.

❺ Lunch at Warung Soba

By now you're ready for some nourishment. Nowhere embodies the Ubud vibe better than **Warung Soba** (Jl Sugriwa 36; meals 30,000-60,000Rp; 🛜🗡). This popular open-air corner place has a daily menu of healthy and vegetarian fare. Most dishes are displayed enticingly, which makes choosing tough.

❻ Shopping Jl Hanoman

Ubud has myriad art shops, clothing boutiques and galleries. Some of the most interesting are found along Jl Hanoman. Take your time wandering this long, slanting street and see what discoveries you make; many shops are owned by the designers of the goods within. Stop in one of the many little cafes for a break.

❼ Yoga Barn

It can seem like every other person in Ubud is either a yoga student or a yoga teacher. Even if you're not yet either, you can get in on the action at the iconic **Yoga Barn** (Map p104, D7; ☏0361-971236; www.balispirit.com; off Jl Raya Pengosekan; classes from 110,000Rp; ⏲7am-8pm), an ever-growing nexus of mellow.

❽ Dance Performance

Ubud has cultural performances virtually every night, and even if you are just visiting for a day, it's well worth staying for an evening performance before heading back to your hotel or villa in the south. One of the best venues is the **Arma Open Stage** (Map p104, D8; ☏0361-976659; Jl Raya Pengosekan) as it attracts some of the best troupes.

For reviews see

⊙	Experiences	p106
⊗	Eating	p109
⊙	Drinking	p113
⊕	Entertainment	p114
⊕	Shopping	p116

500 m
0.25 miles

KUTUH

TAMAN

Jl Sandat

Jl Sriwedan

⊗ 20
Ubud
Lorong Pekandelan
Palace 17
5
Jl Suweta
44
Jl Kajeng
21
49
Jl A-

SAKTI

Museum
Puri
Lukisan 3 ⊙

Jl Raya Ubud

⊙ 39

SAMBAHAN

Campuan Ridge Walk

Sungai Wos

Neka
Art Museum
⊙ 4

Sungai Cerik

CAMPUAN

29 ⊗

⊗ 34
6
Blanco
Renaissance
Museum

31 ⊗

Bali Botanica
Day Spa 9 ⊙

33 ⊗

15 ⊗

Jl Raya Sanggingan

PENESTANAN

Jl Raya Penestanan

⊗ 28

Sungai Blangsuh

Intuitive
Flow
12 ⊙

✕ 19
✕ 22

Jl Pelitan

36 ▣
Jl Raya Ubud

▣ 43
Jl Sukma

Jl Pelitan

▣ 46

✕ 18
Jl Sugriwa

PADANGTEGAL

Nur Salon

▣ 45
Jl Jembawan

Ubud Wellness Spa

⊙ 27
⊙ 25
▣ 13

✕ 32
Jl Goutama

✕ 24
⊙ 11

✕ 30
23
Jl Karna

48 ▣

42 ✕
Gang Beji

▣ 37

Jl Hanoman

PENGOSEKAN

10 ⊙
Yoga Barn

10 ⊙

⊙ 8 Arma

Agung Rai
Jl Made Lebah
Museum of Art

14 ⊙

Jl Raya Pengosekan

▣ 49

▣ 50

✕ 35

✕ 26

Taksu Spa

⊙ Casa Luna
Cooking
School 7

Jl Bisma

38 ⊙

47 ▣

Monkey Forest Rd
(Jl Wanara Wana)

Sacred Monkey
Forest Sanctuary

⊙ 2

Jl Nyuhbulan

NYUHKUNING

Sungai Wos

Experiences

Agung Rai Museum of Art

GALLERY

1 ⊙ Map p104, D8

Founded by Agung Rai as a museum, gallery and cultural centre, the impressive ARMA is the only place in Bali to see haunting works by influential German artist Walter Spies, alongside many more masterpieces. The museum is housed in several traditional buildings set in gardens with water coursing through channels. (Arma; ☎0361-976 659; www.armabali.com; Jl Raya Pengosekan; admission 50,000Rp; ☺9am-6pm, Balinese dancing 3-5pm Mon-Fri, classes 10am Sun)

Sacred Monkey Forest Sanctuary

PARK

2 ⊙ Map p104, C7

This cool and dense swathe of jungle, officially called Mandala Wisata Wanara

☑ Top Tip

Ubud Information

Bali's best visitor centre, **Ubud Tourist Information** (Yaysan Bina Wisata; ☎0361-973285; Jl Raya Ubud; ☺8am-8pm) can answer most questions and has up-to-date information on ceremonies and traditional performances held in the area. Picking up the weekly schedule of performances is essential. Dance tickets are sold here and it often arranges transport to the outlying venues.

Wana, houses three holy temples. The sanctuary is inhabited by a band of grey-haired and greedy long-tailed Balinese macaques who are nothing like the innocent looking doe-eyed monkeys on the brochures.

Nestled in the forest, the interesting **Pura Dalem Agung** has a real Indiana Jones feel to it with the entrance to the inner temple featuring Rangda figures devouring children. (Mandala Wisata Wanara Wana; ☎0361-971304; www.monkeyforest ubud.com; Monkey Forest Rd; adult/child 30,000/20,000Rp; ☺8.30am-6pm)

Museum Puri Lukisan

MUSEUM

3 ⊙ Map p104, C4

This museum displays fine examples of all schools of Balinese art. Just look at the lush composition of *Balinese Market* by Anak Agung Gde Sobrat to see the vibrancy of local painting.

The museum's collection is well curated and labelled in English. The museum has a good bookshop and a cafe. The lush, garden-like grounds alone are worth a visit. (Museum of Fine Arts; ☎0361-975136; www.museumpurilukisan.com; off Jl Raya Ubud; adult/child 75,000Rp/free; ☺9am-5pm)

Neka Art Museum

GALLERY

4 ⊙ Map p104, B1

Quite distinct from Neka Gallery, the Neka Art Museum is the creation of Suteja Neka, a private collector and dealer in Balinese art. It has an excellent and diverse collection and is a good place to learn about the development of painting in Bali. You can get an

Stone dragon, Blanco Renaissance Museum

overview of the myriad local painting styles in the Balinese Painting Hall. Look for the *wayang* (Javanese theatre) works. (☏0361-975074; www.museumneka.com; Jl Raya Sanggingan; adult/child 50,000Rp/free; ⏰9am-5pm Mon-Sat, noon-5pm Sun)

Ubud Palace
PALACE

5 Map p104, D4

The palace and **Puri Saren Agung** share space in the heart of Ubud. The compound was mostly built after the 1917 earthquake and the local royal family still lives here. You can wander around most of the large compound exploring the many traditional, though not excessively ornate, buildings. (cnr Jl Raya Ubud & Jl Suweta; ⏰8am-7pm)

Blanco Renaissance Museum
ART MUSEUM

6 Map p104, B4

The picture of Antonio Blanco mugging with Michael Jackson says it all. His former home and namesake museum captures the artist's theatrical spirit. Blanco came to Bali from Spain via the Philippines. He specialised in erotic art, illustrated poetry and playing the role of an eccentric artist à la Dalí. He died in 1999. More prosaically, enjoy the waterfall on the way in and good views over the river. (☏0361-975502; www.blancomuseum.com; Jl Raya Campuan; admission 80,000Rp; ⏰9am-5pm)

Casa Luna Cooking School

COOKING

7 ⦿ Map p104, C5

There are regular cooking courses at Honeymoon Guesthouse and/or Casa Luna. Half-day courses cover ingredients, cooking techniques and the cultural background of the Balinese kitchen (not all visit the market). Tours are also offered, including a good one to the Gianyar night market. (☏0361-973282; www.casalunabali.com; Honeymoon Guesthouse, Jl Bisma; classes from 350,000Rp; ⊙8am-1.30pm Mon-Sat)

Arma

CULTURAL

8 ⦿ Map p104, D8

A cultural powerhouse offering classes in painting, woodcarving and batik. Other courses include Balinese history, Hinduism and architecture. (☏0361-976659; www.armabali.com; Jl Raya Pengosekan; classes from US$44; ⊙9am-6pm)

Bali Botanica Day Spa

SPA

9 ⦿ Map p104, B1

Set beautifully on a lush hillside past little fields of rice and ducks, this spa offers a range of treatments including Ayurvedic ones. Like a good pesto, the herbal massage is popular. Will provide transport. (☏0361-976739; www.balibotanica.com; Jl Raya Sanggingan; massages from 155,000Rp; ⊙9am-9pm)

Yoga Barn

YOGA

10 ⦿ Map p104, D7

The chakra for the yoga revolution in Ubud, the Yoga Barn sits in its own lotus position amid trees back near a river valley. The name exactly describes what you'll find: a huge range of classes in yoga, Pilates, dance and life-affirming offshoots are held through the week. Owner Meghan Pappenheim also organises the popular Bali Spirit Festival. (☏0361-971236; www.balispirit.com; off Jl Raya Pengosekan; classes from 110,000Rp; ⊙7am-8pm)

Taksu Spa

SPA

11 ⦿ Map p104, D5

Somewhat hidden, yet still in the heart of Ubud, Taksu has a long and rather lavish menu of treatments, as well as a strong focus on yoga. There are private rooms for couples massages, a healthy cafe and a range of classes. (☏0361-971490; www.taksuspa.com; Jl Goutama; massages from 350,000Rp; ⊙9am-9pm; 🛜)

☑ Top Tip

Day-Trip Delirium

As Ubud's popularity grows, the number of day-trippers is proliferating. Unfortunately most are dumped by their over-large tour buses at the corner by the Art Market and left to ponder the hordes of vendors selling the same tat found everywhere else. It's easy to wander about aimlessly and wonder what all the fuss is about. Although Ubud is best experienced over a couple of days and nights, you can get a sense of the place by following our day-long stroll (p102), which covers some of Ubud's essential elements.

Intuitive Flow

YOGA

12 ⊙ Map p104, A3

A lovely yoga studio up amid the rice fields – although just climbing the concrete stairs to get here from Campuan may leave you too spent for a round of asanas. Has workshops in healing arts. (☎0361-977824; www.intuitiveflow.com; Penestanan; yoga classes from 100,000Rp; ⊙classes 9am daily, 4pm Mon-Fri)

Nur Salon

SPA

13 ⊙ Map p104, D5

In a traditional Balinese compound filled with labelled medicinal plants, Nur offers a long menu of straightforward spa and salon services. (☎0361-975352; www.nursalonubud.com; Jl Hanoman 28; 1hr massages 155,000Rp; ⊙9am-9pm)

Ubud Wellness Spa

SPA

14 ⊙ Map p104, D8

A spa that concentrates on what counts, not the fru-fru. A favourite among Ubud's creative community. (☎0361-970493; www.ubudwellness-balispa.com; off Jl Pengosekan; massages from 150,000Rp; ⊙9am-10pm)

Eating

Warung Pulau Kelapa

INDONESIAN $

15 ✖ Map p104, B2

Kelapa has stylish takes on Indonesian classics plus more unusuual dishes from around the archipelago. The surrounds

Q Local Life

Ubud's Library

The **Pondok Pecak Library & Learning Centre** (☎0361-976194; Monkey Forest Rd; classes per hour from 100,000Rp; ⊙9am-5pm Mon-Sat, 1-5pm Sun), on the east side of the football field, is a relaxed place with a children's book section, a pleasant reading area on the roof, a lending library and a range of cultural and language courses on offer. It's a good place to refill your water bottle rather than buy another.

are stylish as well: plenty of whitewash and antiques. Terrace tables across the wide expanse of grass are best. (☎0361-821 5502; Jl Raya Sanggingan; mains 20,000-40,000Rp; ⊙11am-11pm)

Anomali Coffee

COFFEE $

16 ✖ Map p104, D5

Local hipsters get their Java from this place which is, well, from Java. Indonesia's answer to Starbucks takes its (excellent) coffee seriously and so does the young crowd that gathers here. A relaxed place filled with chatter. (Jl Raya Ubud; snacks from 20,000Rp; ⊙7am-11pm; 🛜)

Gelato Secrets

GELATO $

17 ✖ Map p104, D4

Skip the Dairy Queen (yes, really!) on Ubud's main drag in favour of this temple to frozen goodness. Fresh flavours are made from local fruits and spices. (www.gelatosecrets.com; Jl Raya Ubud; treats from 15,000Rp; ⊙11am-11pm)

Bali Buda
CAFE $

18 Map p104, E5

This breezy upper-floor place offers a full range of vegetarian *jamu* (health tonics), salads, sandwiches, savoury crepes, pizzas and gelato. It has a comfy lounging area and is candlelit at night. The bulletin board is packed with idiosyncratic Ubud notices. (☎0361-976324; www.balibuda.com; Jl Jembawan 1; meals from 30,000Rp; ⏰8am-10pm; ✐)

Warung Mangga Madu
INDONESIA $

19 Map p104, E5

The slightly elevated dining terrace here is a fine place to enjoy excellent versions of Indo classics like *nasi campur* (rice with side dishes) That's your driver at the next table reading the *Bali Pos* newspaper. Load up on road snacks to go. (☎0361-977334; Jl Gunung Sari; mains from 15,000Rp; ⏰8am-10pm)

Local Life

Dessert Club

Celebrity chef Will Goldfarb's **Room 4 Dessert** (www.room4dessert.asia; Jl Raya Sanginggan; treats from 100,000Rp; ⏰6pm-late) could be a nightclub except that it just serves desserts, featuring his sweet science and artistry. Get some friends and order the sampler. Pair everything with his classic cocktails and wines and let the night pass by in a sugary glow.

Coffee Studio Seniman
CAFE $

20 Map p104, D4

That 'coffee studio' moniker isn't for show: you see the roasters as you enter this temple of Joe. Take a seat on the large porch and choose from an array of Bali-grown brews. Foods are organic and creative. (☎0361-972085; www.senimancoffee.com; Jl Sriwedari; mains from 40,000Rp; ⏰8am-7pm; 🛜)

Warung Ibu Oka
INDONESIAN $

21 Map p104, D4

Opposite Ubud Palace, you'll see lunchtime crowds waiting for one thing: the Balinese-style roast *babi guling* (suckling pig). Line up for a comparatively pricey version of the Balinese classic. Order a *spesial* to get the best cut. Get there early to avoid day-tripping bus tours. (Jl Suweta; mains from 50,000Rp; ⏰10am-4pm)

Mama's Warung
INDONESIAN $

22 Map p104, E5

A budget find among the bargain homestays of Tebesaya. Mama and her retinue cook up Indo classics that are spicy and redolent with garlic (the avocado salad, yum!). The freshly made peanut sauce for the satay is silky smooth, the fried sambal superb. (Jl Sukma; mains 20,000-40,000Rp; ⏰8am-10pm)

Tutmak Cafe
CAFE $

23 Map p104, D5

The breezy multilevel location here, facing both Jl Dewi Sita and the

Macaques, Sacred Monkey Forest Sanctuary (p106)

football field, is a popular place for a refreshing drink or something to munch on from the menu of Indo classics, salads and sandwiches. Local comers on the make huddle around their laptops plotting their next move. (Jl Dewi Sita; mains 30,000-90,000Rp; ☺8am-11pm; 🛜)

Pica
SOUTH AMERICAN $$

24 🍴 Map p104, D5

Who knew? South American cuisine has travelled well to Ubud, thanks to the young couple behind this excellent restaurant. From the open kitchen, creative dishes making creative use of beef, pork, fish, potatoes and more issue forth in a diner-pleasing stream. The house sourdough bread is superb.

(☏0361-971660; Jl Dewi Sita; mains 70,000-160,000Rp; ☺11am-10pm Tue-Sun)

Waroeng Bernadette
INDONESIAN $$

25 🍴 Map p104, D5

It's not called the 'Home of Rendang' for nothing. The Javanese classic dish of long-marinated meats (beef is the true classic) is pulled off with colour and flair here. Other dishes, such as gado-gado, have a zesty zing missing from lacklustre tourist versions served elsewhere. The elevated dining room is a vision of kitsch. (☏0821 4742 4779; Jl Goutama; mains from 60,000Rp; ☺11am-11pm)

✓ Top Tip

Choosing Galleries

Ubud is dotted with galleries – every street and lane seems to have a place exhibiting artwork for sale. They vary enormously in the choice and quality of items on display. Often you will find local artists in the most unusual places, including your guesthouse. The best way to deal with the plethora of choice is just keep browsing during your Ubud sojourn, gradually sorting out what seems special and what's replicated at every other stall.

Three Monkeys
FUSION $$

26 🍴 Map p104, C6

Have a passionfruit-crush cocktail and settle back amid the frog symphony of the rice fields. Add the glow of tiki torches for a magical effect. By day there are sandwiches, salads and gelato; at night there's a fusion menu of Asian classics. (Monkey Forest Rd; meals from 80,000Rp; ⏰8am-10pm)

Melting Wok
ASIAN $$

27 🍴 Map p104, D5

Pan-Asian fare pleases the masses at this very popular open-air restaurant on the Goutama strip. Curries, noodle dishes, tempeh and a lot more fill a menu that makes decisions tough. Desserts take on a bit of colonial flavour: French accents abound. The service is relaxed but efficient. Bookings advised. (☎0361-929 9716; Jl Goutama; mains from 50,000Rp; ⏰10am-11pm Tue-Sun)

Alchemy
VEGAN $$

28 🍴 Map p104, B4

This place could be called Oxymoron's given that we're not sure what 'Raw Vegan Ice Cream' is, although we do know it's good. This prototypical Ubud restaurant has a vast customised salad menu as well as cashew-milk drinks, durian smoothies, fennel juice and a lot more. The raw-chocolate desserts are addictive. (☎0361-971981; Jl Raya Penestanan 75; mains from 50,000Rp; ⏰7am-9pm)

Elephant
VEGETARIAN $$

29 🍴 Map p104, B2

High-concept vegetarian dining with gorgeous views across the Sungai Cerik valley. They do pleasurable things with potatoes here – and lots of other vegetables. Foods are well-seasoned, interesting and topped off with an especially good dessert menu. It's well off the road. (☎0361-716 1907; Jl Raya Sanggingan; mains 40,000-150,000Rp; ⏰8am-9.30pm)

Cafe Havana
LATIN AMERICAN $$

30 🍴 Map p104, D5

All that's missing is Fidel. Actually, the decrepitude of its namesake city is also missing from this smart and stylish cafe. Dishes exude Latin flair, such as the tasty pork numbers, but expect surprises such as the fab crème brûlée oatmeal in the mornings. There's nightly salsa dancing and live music 7pm to 10pm. (☎0361-972973; Jl Dewi Sita; mains from 60,000Rp; ⏰8am-11pm)

Naughty Nuri's

BARBECUE $$

31 Map p104, B1

This legendary expat hangout now has lines waiting for food through the day and night. The grilled steaks, ribs and burgers are popular – proof that a little media hype helps – even if all the chewing needed gets in the way of chatting. The original lures, potent martinis, are as large as ever. (☏0361-977547; Jl Raya Sanggingan; meals from 80,000Rp; ⏰11am-11pm)

Locavore

FUSION $$$

32 Map p104, D5

The foodie heaven in Ubud, this temple to locally sourced, ultra-creative foods is the town's toughest table. Book weeks in advance. Meals come as degustations and can top out at nine courses (expect this cuisine nirvana to last upwards of three hours). Chefs Eelke Plasmeijer and Ray Adriansyah are magicians; enjoy the show. (☏0361-977733; www.restaurantlocavore.com; Jl Dewi Sita; mains from US$30; ⏰noon-2.30pm, 6-10pm Mon-Sat; ❄)

Mozaic

FUSION $$$

33 Map p104, B2

Chef Chris Salans oversees this much-lauded top-end restaurant. Fine French fusion cuisine features on a constantly changing seasonal menu that takes its influences from tropical Asia. Dine in an elegant garden or ornate pavilion. Choose from four tasting menus, one of which is simply a surprise. (☏0361-975768; www.mozaic-bali.com; Jl Raya Sanggingan; menus from 1,250,000Rp; ⏰6-10.30pm)

Bridges

FUSION $$$

34 Map p104, B4

The namesake bridges are right outside this multilevel restaurant with sweeping views of the gorgeous river gorge. You'll hear the rush of the water over rocks far below while you indulge in a top-end cocktail on the rocks or choose from the mix of Asian and European fusion fare. Popular happy-hour drink specials. (☏0361-970095; www.bridges-bali.com; Jl Raya Campuan; mains US$15-35; ⏰11am-11.30pm, happy hour 4-7pm)

Drinking

Laughing Buddha

CAFE

35 Map p104, C6

People crowd the street at night in front of this small cafe with live music Monday through Saturday nights. Rock, blues, vocals and more. The kitchen is open late for Asian bites (meals 40,000Rp to 70,000Rp). (☏0361-970928; Monkey Forest Rd; ⏰9am-midnight; 📶)

Jazz Café

BAR

36 Map p104, E5

Ubud's most popular nightspot (and that's not faint praise although competition might be lacking), Jazz Café turns on a relaxed atmosphere amid a charming garden of coconut palms and ferns. The menu features Asian-fusion dishes; there is live music most nights. (☏0361-976594; www.jazzcafebali.com; Jl Sukma 2; ⏰5-11.30pm Tue-Sun, to 12.30am Sat)

Lebong Cafe

BAR

37 Map p104, C5

Get up, stand up, stand up for your... reggae. This nightlife hub stays open until at least midnight, with live reggae and rock most nights. A few other places good for drinks are nearby. (Monkey Forest Rd; ☺11am-midnight)

Napi Orti

BAR

38 Map p104, C6

This upstairs place is your best bet for a late-night drink. Get boozy under the hazy gaze of Jim Morrison and Sid Vicious. (Monkey Forest Rd; drinks from 12,000Rp; ☺noon-late)

Entertainment

Pura Dalem Ubud

DANCE

39 Map p104, C4

At the west end of Jl Raya Ubud, this open-air venue has a flamelit carved-stone backdrop, and in many ways is the most evocative place to see a dance performance. (Jl Raya Ubud)

Understand

Dance Troupes: Good & Bad

All dance groups on Ubud's stages are not created equal. You've got true artists with international reputations and then you've got some who really shouldn't quit their day jobs. If you're a Balinese dance novice, you shouldn't worry too much about this; just pick a venue and go.

But after a few performances, you'll start to appreciate the differences in talent, and that's part of the enjoyment. Clue: if the costumes are dirty, the orchestra seems particularly uninterested and you find yourself watching a dancer and saying 'I could do that', then the group is B-grade.

Excellent troupes that regularly perform in Ubud include the following:

▶ **Semara Ratih** High-energy, creative Legong interpretations. The best local troupe musically.

▶ **Gunung Sari** Legong dance; one of Bali's oldest and most respected troupes.

▶ **Semara Madya** Kecak dance; especially good for the hypnotic chants. A mystical experience for some.

▶ **Tirta Sari** Legong and barong dance.

▶ **Cudamani** One of Bali's best gamelan troupes. They rehearse in Pengosekan.

Understand

Spas, Yoga, Healers & More

Ubud brims with salons and spas where you can heal, pamper, rejuvenate or otherwise focus on your personal needs, both physical and mental. The larger hotels and resorts all have in-house spas, which are often quite lavish. There are also all manner of independent spas, which range from the sybaritic to the no-nonsense. At the latter you may find that the pleasure comes well after the pain. In addition, Ubud is home to all manner of practitioners. You can get an idea of what's available by perusing the enormous bulletin board outside Bali Buda (p110).

Yoga

Demand for yoga in Ubud seems virtually unquenchable. Fortunately there is a plethora of studios, instructors and classes available. The **Bali Spirit Festival** (www.balispiritfestival.com; ☉early Apr) celebrates yoga, good living and spiritual health with concerts, seminars and classes over several days.

Traditional Healers

Bali's traditional healers, known as *balian* (*dukun* on Lombok), play an important part in Bali's culture by treating physical and mental illness, removing spells and channelling information from the ancestors. Many are found in Ubud. Utilising techniques that are far removed from Western medicine, *balian* offer spiritual and physical healing.

Consider the following before a visit:

▶ Make an appointment before visiting a *balian*.

▶ Know that English is rarely spoken.

▶ Dress respectfully (long trousers and a shirt or better a sarong and sash).

▶ Women should not be menstruating.

▶ Never point your feet at the healer.

▶ Bring an offering into which you have tucked the consulting fee, which will range from 100,000Rp to 250,000Rp per person.

▶ Understand what you're getting into: your treatment will be very public and probably painful. It may include deep tissue massage, being poked with sharp sticks or having chewed herbs spat on you.

Finding a *balian* can take some work. Ask at your hotel, which can probably help with making an appointment.

Pura Taman Saraswati
DANCE

40 ⭐ Map p104, C4

The beauty of the setting may distract you from the dancers, although at night you can't see the lily pads and lotus flowers that are such an attraction by day. (Ubud Water Palace; Jl Raya Ubud)

Ubud Palace
DANCE

Performances are held here almost nightly against a beautiful backdrop in the palace (see 5 ◉ Map p104, D4). (Jl Raya Ubud)

Padangtegal Kaja
DANCE

41 ⭐ Map p104, D5

A simple, open venue in a very convenient location. In many ways this location hints at what dance performances have looked like in Ubud for generations. (Jl Hanoman)

Arma Open Stage
DANCE

Arma has some of the best troupes (see 8 ◉ Map p104; D8). (☎0361-976659; Jl Raya Pengosekan)

Shopping

Tin Parrot
CLOTHING

42 🔒 Map p104, D5

The trademark parrot of this T-shirt shop is a characterful bird and he (she?) appears in many guises on this shop's line of custom T-shirts. Designs range from cool to groovy to offbeat. Everything is made from high-quality cotton that's been pre-shrunk. (www.tnparrot.com; Jl Dewi Sita; ⏱10am-8pm)

Ganesha Bookshop
BOOKS

43 🔒 Map p104, E5

Ubud's best bookshop has an amazing amount of stock jammed into a small space: an excellent selection of Indonesian studies, travel, arts, music, fiction (including used titles) and maps. Good staff recommendations. (www.ganesha booksbali.com; Jl Raya Ubud; ⏱10am-8pm)

Threads of Life Indonesian Textile Arts Center
TEXTILES

44 🔒 Map p104, D4

This small store is part of a foundation that works to preserve traditional textile creation in Balinese villages. There's a small but visually stunning collection of exquisite handmade fabrics in stock. (☎0361-972187; www.threadsoflife.com; Jl Kajeng 24; ⏱10am-7pm)

*Asterisk
JEWELLERY

45 🔒 Map p104, D5

Custom and artistically designed silver jewellery. The designs here are delicate and almost wistful. (☎0361-749 1770; www. asterisk-shop.com; Jl Hanoman; ⏱10am-8pm)

Moari
MUSICAL INSTRUMENTS

46 🔒 Map p104, E5

New and restored Balinese musical instruments are sold here. Splurge on a cute little bamboo flute for 30,000Rp. (☎0361-977367; Jl Raya Ubud; ⏱10am-8pm)

PETER STUCKINGS/GETTY IMAGES ©

Ubud Palace

Goddess on the Go!   CLOTHING

47 🔒 Map p104, C6

A large selection of women's clothes for adventure, made to be comfortable, easy-to-pack and ecofriendly. (📞0361-976084; Monkey Forest Rd; ⏰10am-8pm)

Kou   BEAUTY

48 🔒 Map p104, D5

Luxurious locally handmade organic soaps perfume your nose as you enter. Put one in your undies drawer and smell fine for weeks. The range is unlike that found in chain stores selling luxe soap. (📞0361-971905; Jl Dewi Sita; ⏰10am-8pm)

Namaste   NEW AGE

49 🔒 Map p104, D7

Just the place to buy a crystal to get your spiritual house in order, Namaste is a gem of a store with a range of New Age supplies. Incense, yoga mats, moody instrumental music – it's all here. (📞0361-796 9178; Jl Hanoman 64; ⏰10am-8pm)

Pondok Bamboo Music Shop   MUSICAL INSTRUMENTS

50 🔒 Map p104, D7

Hear the music of a thousand bamboo wind chimes at this store owned by noted gamelan musician Nyoman Warsa, who offers music lessons and stages shadow-puppet shows. (📞0361-974807; Monkey Forest Rd; ⏰10am-8pm)

Explore

East Bali

Some of the lushest land in Bali is found in the east. Ancient rice terraces spill down the sides of hills into wide river valleys. Long beaches in the west give way to smaller hidden ones in the east. Padangbai is a port town with a real traveller vibe while Semarapura has important relics from Bali's royal past.

The Region in a Day

East Bali makes a splendid day trip from both south Bali and Ubud. Start your day watching for the towering Gunung Agung, the island's most sacred volcano. Clouds usually obscure it in the heat of the day. While it's still cool, drive the **Sidemen Road** (p121) and maybe stop for a rice field ramble. Or you might plunge into the family fun of **Bali Safari & Marine Park** (p123).

For lunch, try one of the choices along the coast road such as local fave **Merta Sari** (p124) or the fabulous fare and luxe surrounds of **Terrace** (p124). After lunch, take time at a beach such as **Pasir Putih** (p122) or one of the many black-sand beaches towards Sanur. Wander historic **Semarapura** (p121) and **Taman Kertha Gosa** (p125); check out the local markets.

Day-trippers will want to be back home by dark. But if you're staying, **Padangbai** (p121) has an alluringly mellow beach vibe. Otherwise, resorts and hotels great and small are scattered along the coast and near Sidemen.

♥ Best of Bali

Snorkelling
Padangbai (p121)

Surfing
Pantai Keramas (p123)

Beaches
Lebih Beach (p122)

Pasir Putih (p122)

Eating
Gianyar Babi Guleng (p123)

For Kids
Bali Safari & Marine Park (p123)

❶ Getting There & Around

🚗 Car From south Bali or Ubud you can arrange a car and driver for about US$50 per day to go touring in the east.

Walk Within Semarapura and Pandangbai you can easily walk between sights. However, you'll need transport to get from one part to another of this large region.

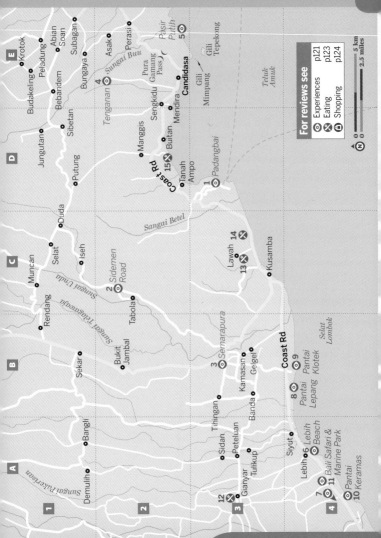

E

Krotok
Budakeling
Peladung
Abian Soan
Subagan
Asak
Bungaya
Perasi
Pasir Putih
5
Gili Tepekong

Bebandem
Sibetan
Tenganan
Sungai Buu
4
Pura Gamang Pass
Sengkidu
Candidasa
Gili Mimpang

Jungutan
Putung
Manggis
Buitan
Mendira
15
Tanah Ampo
1
Padangbai
Teluk Amuk

For reviews see
⊙ Experiences   p121
✕ Eating   p123
🛍 Shopping   p124

5 km
2.5 miles

Duda
Sangai Betel

D

Selat
Iseh
14
Lawah
13
Kusamba

Muncan
Sidemen Road
2
Tabola

C

Rendang
Sungai Unda
Sungai Telaga Waja
Bukit Jambal

Selat Lombok

Sekar
3
Semarapura
Coast Rd
9
Pantai Klotek

B

Bangli
Kamasan
Gelgel
Banda
8
Pantai Lepang

Demulih
Sungai Pakerisan
Thingan
Sidan
Peteluan
Siyut
6
Lebih Beach

A

Gianyar
Tulikup
Lebih
12
11
Bali Safari & Marine Park
7
Pantai Keramas
10

1

2

3

4

Weaver, Tenganan village (p122)

Experiences

Padangbai TOWN

 1 Map p120, D3

Bali's eastern port city makes a good base for exploration. You can relax on the beach with a beer while watching the Lombok ferry come and go or head just over a knoll to the light-sand Blue Lagoon Beach, which is a good place to snorkel. The cool traveller vibe makes this a good choice for an overnight stop.

Sidemen Road SCENIC DRIVE

2 Map p120, C2

Sidemen has a spectacular location and the road that runs through it may be the most beautiful in Bali (start at Semarapura, end near Duda). There are many walks through the rice fields and streams in the multihued green valley that forms what could be an amphitheatre for the gods. Little guesthouses sit amid the splendour.

Semarapura TOWN

3 Map p120, B3

Besides its history, Semarapura is a good place to stroll and get a feel for modern Balinese life. The markets are large and offer a vast range of Balinese goods, yet a dearth of tourists keeps the mood authentic. Glittery gold shops vie with plastic emporiums for shoppers' attention; a profusion of fruit is everywhere.

Local Life
Bali's Bat Cave

One of Bali's most important temples, **Pura Goa Lawah** (Bat Cave Temple; Jl Raya Goa Lawa; adult/child 10,000/5000Rp; car park 2000Rp; ☺8am-6pm) is 3km east of Kusamba on the road to Padangbai. The cave in the cliff face is packed full of bats, and the complex is equally over-crowded with tour groups. Legend says the cave leads all the way to Pura Besakih, some 19km away.

Tenganan   VILLAGE

4 ◉ Map p120, E2

Bali's oldest inhabitants are the Bali Aga people, who lead separate lives to Hindu Bali. Tenganan, their spiritual home, is surrounded by a wall that protects the village from outside influences. Not *all* outside influences, mind you, as the Aga have found profits in accepting visitors, albeit quite gently. Tenganan is 4km off the coast road just west of Candidasa.

Pasir Putih   BEACH

5 ◉ Map p120, E2

The name of this idyllic white-sand beach, backed by coconut trees, means 'White Sand'. Simple thatched cafes offer snacks and cold Bintangs. Access is an adventure: 5.6km east of Candidasa, follow a paved track off the main road for 1.5km to a temple, where locals will collect a fee. The beach is another 600m down a very bad road.

Lebih Beach   BEACH

6 ◉ Map p120, A4

Lebih Beach has glittering mica-infused sand. Just off the main road, the large Sungai Pakerisan (Pakerisan River), which starts near Tampaksiring, reaches the sea near here. Fishing boats line the shore, which is fitting as there's a strip of warungs with specialities that include fish satay and rich seafood soup. The air is redolent with the smell of BBQ fish; this is an excellent stop for lunch.

Pantai Purnama   BEACH

7 ◉ Map p120, A4

Small, but has the blackest sand, reflecting billions of sparkles in the sunlight. Religion is big here. The temple, Pura Erjeruk, is important for irrigation of rice fields, while some of Bali's most elaborate full-moon purification ceremonies are held here each month. Villas are appearing.

Pantai Lepang   BEACH

8 ◉ Map p120, B4

Worth visiting just for the little slice of rural Bali you pass through on the 600m drive from the main road. Rice and corn grow in profusion. Down at the carbon-coloured sand you'll find small dunes, no shade, a couple of vendors and a lot of reasons to snap some pics. A sign explains that this is a sea turtle sanctuary. Conversely, that huge development you see nearby is the Tamansari Jivva time-share condo development.

Pantai Klotek
BEACH

9 ◎ Map p120, B4

The lovely 800m drive along the hilly road off the coast road is but a prelude to this very interesting beach. The quiet at the temple, Pura Batu Klotek, belies its great significance: sacred statues are brought here from Pura Besakih for ritual cleansing. Look for a *bakso ayam* (chicken soup) cart; the owner makes fresh noodles by hand all day. Admire the pale blue flowers – they're sacred – on the wild midori shrubs here.

Pantai Keramas
BEACH

10 ◎ Map p120, A4

Will this be the next Echo Beach (the popular beach and surf break near Canggu)? Villa and hotel projects are sprouting here. The surf is consistent and world-class. **Komune Bali** (☏0361-301 8888; www.komuneresorts.com; Jl Pantai Keramas; r from US$90; ❄ 🛜 ⛵) is a high-profile surf resort that has erected light towers for night-surfing, which has proven hugely popular. Despite this, the hotel has actually done a good job of trying to blend into the existing landscape. It has a very attractive pool area and a cafe in the dune up from the high-tide line.

Bali Safari & Marine Park
AMUSEMENT PARK

11 ◎ Map p120, A4

Kids love Bali Safari and Marine Park and their parents are happy they love someplace. This big-ticket animal-theme park is filled with critters whose species never set foot in Bali until their cage door opened. Displays are large and naturalistic. A huge menu of extra-cost options includes animal rides and a night safari. Visitors should note that the park stages animal shows that include elephants: animal welfare advocates claim that these are unnatural and harmful for the animals. (☏0361-950000; www.balisafari marinepark.com; Prof Dr Ida Bagus Mantra Bypass; adult/child from US$49/39; ⊙9am-5pm, Bali Agung show 2.30pm Tue-Sun)

Sobek
RAFTING

◎

Offers popular whitewater rafting trips on the Sungai Telagawaja, a river that cuts through a beautiful swath of east Bali. (☏0361-729 016; www.balisobek.com; adult/child US$79/52)

Eating

Gianyar Babi Guleng
BALINESE $

12 🍴 Map p120, A3

People come to Gianyar to sample the market food, like the *babi guling* (spit-roast pig stuffed with chilli, turmeric, garlic and ginger). Although scoring a zero for naming imagination, this open-air shopfront scores a 10 for its *babi*, which is first among much competition. It's on a tiny side street at the west end of the centre. (meals from 20,000Rp; ⊙7am-4pm)

Merta Sari INDONESIAN $

13 🍴 Map p120, C3

Follow the crowds of Balinese to this open-air pavilion that's famous for its *nasi campur*. This version includes juicy pounded fish satay, a slightly sour, fragrant fish broth, fish steamed in banana leaves, snake beans in a fragrant tomato-peanut sauce and a fiery red sambal. (Bingin; meals from 25,000Rp; ⊙10am-3pm)

Sari Baruna INDONESIAN $

14 🍴 Map p120, C3

Sari Baruna grills fish with attitude and authority. It's in a rickety bamboo hut about 200m west of Pura Goa Lawah. (Jl Raya Goa Lawa; meals 20,000Rp; ⊙10am-6pm)

Topi Inn CAFE $

Juices, shakes and coffee are served here (see 1 ◉ Map p120, D3) throughout the day. Breakfasts are big, and whatever is landed by the fishing boats during the day is grilled by night Refill your water bottle here for 2000Rp. (☎0363-41424; Jl Silayukti; mains 20,000-40,000Rp; ⊙8am-10pm)

Terrace FUSION $$

15 🍴 Map p120, D2

One of Bali's finest hotels is hidden along the jutting cliffs about 5km beyond the Padangbai turn-off. The architecture includes three pools that step down to the sea in shades of blue. Above this, the superb Terrace is the resort's casual cafe and has a creative menu showing global and local influences. (☎0363-41333; www. amankila.com; lunches US$10-25; ⊙8am-5pm)

◎ Local Life
Tasty Night Market

The sound of hundreds of cooking pots adds a frenetic and festive clamour to Gianyar's **Night Market** (Jl Ngurah Rai; ⊙5-11pm), which any local will tell you has some of the best food in Bali. Scores of stalls set up each night in the centre and cook up a mouth-watering and jaw-dropping range of dishes. It's a 20-minute drive from Ubud.

Shopping

Cap Togog TEXTILES

This place is on the main drag west of the centre (see 12 🍴 Map p120, A3), 500m apart from the larger **Tenun Ikat Setia Cili** (☎0361-943409; Jl Astina Utara; ⊙9am-5pm). Unlike its competitor, Cap Togog has a fascinating production area below; follow the sounds of dozens of clacking wooden looms. (☎0361-943046; Jl Astina Utara 11; ⊙8am-5pm)

Semarapura Market MARKET

Semarapura's sprawling market is one of the best in east Bali. Semarapura (see 3 ◉ Map p120, B3) a vibrant hub of commerce and the market is a meeting place for people of the region. You can easily spend an hour wandering about the warren of stalls on three levels. It's grimy, yes, but also endlessly fascinating. Huge straw baskets of lemons, limes, tomatoes and other produce are islands of colour amid the chaos. A plethora of locally made snacks are offered in profusion; try several. (Jl Diponegoro; ⊙6am-8pm)

Understand

Semarapura & Bali's History

From the 14th to the 16th centuries, Gegel, a town very close to today's Semarapura, was the centre of power on Bali. In the 1700s, however, internal squabbling diluted the local royalty's influence, and royals from other parts of Bali vied for power.

Still, in 1849 the rulers of Klungkung (which had superseded Gegel as the royal centre and is today called Semarapura) and Gianyar defeated a Dutch invasion force at Kusamba. Before the Dutch could launch a counter-attack, a force from Tabanan arrived and the trader Mads Lange was able to broker a peace settlement.

The Suicidal Last Stand

For the next 50 years the south Bali kingdoms squabbled, until the rajah of Gianyar petitioned the Dutch for support. When the Dutch finally invaded the south, the king of Klungkung had a choice between a suicidal *puputan,* like the rajah of Denpasar, or an ignominious surrender, as Tabanan's rajah had done. He chose the former. In April 1908, as the Dutch surrounded his palace, Taman Kertha Gosa, the Dewa Agung and hundreds of his relatives and followers marched out to certain death from Dutch gunfire or the blades of their own kris (traditional daggers). Klungkung (Semarapura) was the last Balinese kingdom to succumb and the sacrifice is commemorated in the large Puputan Monument. Locals still have great pride in the toughness of their ancestors.

Taman Kertha Gosa

This **palace** (Jl Puputan; adult/child 12,000/6000Rp, parking 2000Rp; ☻6am-6pm) was established in 1710 when the Dewa Agung dynasty moved to today's Semarapura from nearby Gegel. It was laid out as a large square, believed to be in the form of a mandala, with courtyards, gardens, pavilions and moats. Most of the original palace and grounds were destroyed by Dutch attacks in 1908 – the elaborately carved gateway on the south side of the square is all that remains of the palace itself. However, the Kertha Gosa, the old royal court, survives and is a splendid example of open-air Balinese architecture. While wandering the gardens, save time for the good little museum.

Top Experiences
Gili Trawangan

Getting There

⚓ **Boat** Gili Cat (www.gilicat.com) leaves from Padangbai; Blue Water Express (www.bluewater-express.com) from Serangan and Padangbai. Rates are US$50 to US$60 one way; the trip takes about two hours.

Gili Trawangan's main drag boasts a glittering roster of lounge bars, hip hotels and cosmopolitan restaurants, mini-marts and dive schools. And yet, behind this glitzy facade, a bohemian character endures, with rickety warungs and reggae joints surviving between the cocktail tables. Fast boats have brought Gili T close to Bali and, for many, a night or two partying here, and enjoying its beautiful waters in between, is an essential part of their trip.

Gili Trawangan

Don't Miss

Beaches

Gili T is almost completely ringed with sand, and on the east side of the island, where most of the action is, this sand is among the nicest in Indonesia. Think pearly white grains lapped by azure blue waters. Oh, yes.

Snorkelling

Surrounded by coral reefs and with easy beach access, Gili T offers superb snorkelling. If you enjoy swimming, there's no better feeling than exploring a reef without the burden of a tank on your back. You can start on any beach or go further out on one of many glass-bottomed boats. Besides the many fish, it's common to see sea turtles.

Diving

The Gili Islands are a superb dive destination as the marine life is plentiful and varied. Turtles and black- and white-tip reef sharks are common, and the macro life is excellent, with sea horses, pipefish and lots of crustaceans. Around the full moon large schools of bumphead parrotfish appear to feast on coral spawn; at other times manta rays cruise past dive sites.

Nightlife

Gili T morphs between rave central and boutique chic. Parties are held three nights a week (Monday, Wednesday and Friday), shifting between venues. DJs mix house, trance and increasingly some R 'n' B as the scene becomes more commercial. The island has more than a dozen great beachside drinking dens, ranging from sleek lounge bars to simple shacks.

☑ Top Tips

▶ Gili T's neighbours, Gili Meno and Gili Air, are much quieter, with a fraction of Gili T's nightlife.

▶ There are fly-by-night boat operators to the Gilis and there have been accidents; stick with the experienced companies.

▶ Gili Trawangan has ATMs.

▶ During Ramadan, nightlife is curtailed out of respect for local culture.

✗ Take a Break

Enjoying a prime beachfront location, **Scallywags** (☎0370-614 5301; www.scallywags resort.com; meals 40,000-180,000Rp; ⏱8am-10pm; ⏱) has tables under Arabian-style canvas and an attractive shabby-chic interior. Specials are chalked up daily on blackboards. The menu covers everything from freshly grilled fish to pasta, panini and wraps to big breakfasts.

The Best of
Bali

Beach huts
TOM BONAVENTURE/GETTY IMAGES ©

Best Walks
Ayung River Valley

🏃 The Walk

The wonders of the Ayung River (Sungai Ayung) are the focus of this outing, which may be close to Ubud but is a world away in terms of its pure tropical splendour. You'll walk in a lush valley past a rushing river amid impossibly green vistas. Along the way you'll pass through an iconically typical village and you'll cross through the old compound of one of Bali's greatest expat writers.

Start Campuan Bridge

Finish Campuan Bridge

Length 5km; five hours

✕ Take a Break

There are no breaks in the valley! Bring plenty of water and assemble a picnic from a deli or cafe in Ubud. But towards the end of your walk, options for a pause abound. The cafes line up like a string of oases as you make your way blessedly downhill on Jl Raya Sanggingan.

MANFRED GOTTSCHALK/LONELY PLANET IMAGES ©

Local women preparing for a festival, Penestanan

❶ Penestanan

From the Campuan bridge, climb the steep concrete stairs opposite the Hotel Tjampuhan and walk west past rice fields and artists' studios to the village of **Penestanan**. You'll see more artists' studios and traditional family compounds. Look for the small temple that always graces a corner.

❷ Sayan

Now head north on a small road that curves around to **Sayan** and the **Sayan Terrace hotel**. This was the site of Colin McPhee's home in the 1930s, as chronicled in his excellent book *A House in Bali* (available at island bookshops). He was one of the first Westerners to take a scholarly approach to documenting Bali's music and dance.

❸ Path into the Valley

Follow the downhill path before the gate to the hotel's rooms. It's steep and can be slippery, plus there are offshoots that can lead you astray; locals will help you find your way down for a tip of 10,000Rp.

❹ Ayung River Valley

Following the rough trails north, along the eastern side of the **Ayung**, you traverse steep slopes, cross paddy fields and pass irrigation canals through dense tropical jungle. You don't need to follow any specific trail as you head slowly north along the river. Water plunges over huge boulders and eddies in cool-looking pools.

❺ Kedewatan

After about 1.5km of meandering through the river valley (take your time, wander about, see what you discover) you'll reach the finish point for white-water rafting trips that start further upriver. Under a dense canopy of trees, take a good but steep trail up to the main road at **Kedewatan**; head north then east about 1km along the main road into Ubud.

❻ Sanggingan

At **Sanggingan** the road curves 90 degrees due south and begins the long, gentle descent to the Campuan Bridge where you started. Among the many cafes along here, you might feel you deserve one of the famous martinis at Naughty Nuri's, or you can stop at the Neka Art Museum to see how artists portrayed many of the sights you've seen.

White-water rafting, Ayung River

MARTIN HARVEY/GETTY IMAGES ©

Best
Beaches

Bali is ringed with beaches, which is one of the reasons all those planes keep landing at the airport. They come in so many forms that there's virtually a beach for everyone. There's a reason that tourism started in Kuta: just look at that beach. It disappears in both directions and has ceaselessly crashing waves, which at their best are long aqua ribbons twisting into white.

FELIX HUG/GETTY IMAGES ©

A Beach for Any Mood

On Sundays Kuta Beach is thronged with locals; on any day massages and cheap beers from coolers are offered along the beach. Holidaymakers claim a part of the beach they like, make friends with the vendors and return to 'their' beach for the rest of their trip.

From Seminyak north through Batubelig, Batu Bolong and on to Echo Beach, hipster hangouts vie with posh clubs and humble beer vendors for business. South of the airport, the vast arid rock that is the Bukit Peninsula shelters a score of beaches hidden in small coves below the cliffs all the way to Ulu Watu. Coming closest to the white-sand cliché, these idylls are good for watching the world-class surfing offshore amid beautiful surrounds.

Meanwhile, in Nusa Dua, Tanjung Benoa and Sanur families frolic on mellow reef-sheltered beaches picked clean daily. East Bali has a swathe of seldom-visited volcanic black-sand beaches while Nusa Lembongan has beach guesthouses with awesome sunset views. Over on Gili T, the sand is white and lined with bars and clubs for a full-on party scene.

☑ **Top Tips**

▶ Although Bali's west-facing beaches from Echo Beach to Ulu Watu offer spectacular sunsets, east-facing ones like Sanur enjoy their own show as Nusa Lembongan and the islands glow pink offshore.

▶ Almost every beach has at least one vendor ready to pull a cold one out of the cooler.

Best for Hanging with Friends

Double Six Beach Fun mix of visitors and locals. (p26)

Gili Trawangan Those raves about the raves are just the start. (p126)

Padang Padang Beach

Seminyak Beach Clubs and cafes great and humble dot the sand. (p37)

Batu Bolong The new hotspot with a cool, all-inclusive scene. (p51)

Balangan Beach Classic cove beach is worth the drive. (p69)

Kuta Beach The original beach still knows how to kick up some sand. (p26)

Echo Beach Gnarly surf action entertains the masses. (p51)

Padang Padang Beach Small enough to be one big scene on busy days. (p69)

Jungutbatu Beach Subscribe to the surfer vibe on Nusa Lembongan. (p91)

Pasir Putih The coolest beach in east Bali, with great cafes. (p122)

Best for Families

Sanur Beach Reefs offshore keep the surf mellow, just like the town. (p86)

Mushroom Bay Small resorts, water sports and a surf-protected site. (p91)

Best for Escaping

Bingin Beach Difficult access makes this the spot not to be spotted. (p69)

Pantai Klotek The sparkles in the black sand outnumber visitors a trillion to one. (p123)

Best
Nightlife

The nightclub scene in Kuta, Legian and Seminyak is one of Bali's biggest draws. The partying starts at beachside bars at sunset and moves to an ever-changing line-up of bars and clubs. Bouncing from one to another all night long is a Bali tradition that guarantees you'll be overheated from the exertion, the music, the booze, the companionship or all of the above.

JEFF HUNTER/GETTY IMAGES ©

Nightlife for Every Taste

You can quaff an ice-cold Bintang at sandy-floored bars with the full tropical cliché. At the other end of the style spectrum there are several scenester clubs that may force you to spend just as much time prepping your look as actually partying.

Mostly, however, nights on Bali are lacking in rules or pretension: on any night you can listen to live rock, dance salsa, see a drag show, cut shapes to a famous DJ set, win (or lose) a shot contest or just have a smashing good time with friends new and old.

Best Partying

Sky Garden Lounge Floor after floor of club and bar action fuelled by drink specials. (p32)

Bounty So low-brow it's a must. (p33)

Gili Trawangan The entire island is renowned for its all-night raves. (p126)

Best Stylish Drinking

Potato Head High-concept lounge and cocktails on the Seminyak sands. (p41)

Red Carpet Champagne Bar Ridiculously over-the-top for fizzy drinks and oysters. (p41)

☑ Top Tip

▶ Enjoying traditional Balinese nightlife may be the best memory of your trip: the dance performances in and around Ubud combine beauty, talent, drama and even comedy.

Best Live Music

Jazz Café Regular live acts belie the rumour that Ubud has no nightlife. (p113)

Bali Jo Bali's best drag shows. (p39)

Mantra Feels like an outdoor venue for gritty live rock, even when there isn't music on. (p41)

Best
Pampering

Whether it's a total fix for the mind, body and spirit, or simply the desire for some quick-fix serenity, many travellers to Bali can happily spend hours (sometimes days) being massaged, scrubbed, perfumed, pampered, bathed and blissed-out. Sometimes this happens on the beach or in a garden, other times in stylish, even lavish surroundings.

MATTHEW WAKEM/GETTY IMAGES ©

Bliss in Every Flavour

Spas may be serious or they may seem frivolous, they can be found down little lanes and in the most exclusive hotels. Treatments are myriad, from the almost sensually relaxing to serious endeavours designed to purge your body and maybe your soul of toxins. You can lie back and enjoy or take active part; yoga is hugely popular. Happily the Balinese have just the right cultural background and disposition to enhance the experience.

Balinese Massage

Traditional Balinese massage techniques of stretching, long strokes, skin rolling and palm and thumb pressure result in a lowering of tension, improved blood flow and circulation, and an all-over feeling of calm. Traditional herbal treatments are popular.

Best Massage

Jari Menari Bali's renowned centre for serious massage. (p38)

Sundari Day Spa Organic massage oils set the mood at this day spa. (p52)

Best Pampering Spa

Prana Utterly lavish in its treatments and opulent in decor. (p38)

Jamu Traditional Spa Popular, serene and posh. (p85)

Bali Botanica Day Spa A little quirky, a little creative, just like Ubud. (p108)

Best Yoga

Yoga Barn *The* centre for all things yoga in Ubud. (p108)

Taksu Spa Combines yoga with spa treatments. (p108)

Desa Seni The south Bali choice for serious yoga. (p52)

Best
Diving & Snorkelling

The chance to stare down a 3m-long sunfish is reason enough to go diving here. These huge creatures are found at many spots around Bali, as are a huge variety of other fish and mammals, from parrotfish to whales. And snorkelling, at spots all around the islands, can be just as rewarding.

REINHARD DIRSCHERL/GETTY IMAGES ©

Diving Bali

With its warm water, extensive coral reefs and abundant marine life, Bali offers excellent diving adventures. Reliable dive schools and operators all around Bali's coasts can train complete beginners or arrange challenging trips that will satisfy most experienced divers. Out on Nusa Lembongan, you'll find top-notch dive operators who can take you to sites there and at neighbouring Nusa Penida – a world-class dive location. Gili T provides equally excellent opportunities.

If you're not picky, you'll find all the equipment you need (the quality, size and age of the equipment can vary). If you provide your own, you can usually get a discount on your dive. Some small, easy-to-carry things to bring from home include protective gloves, spare mask straps, silicone lubricant and extra globes (bulbs) for your torch (flashlight).

Snorkelling Bali

Snorkelling gear is available near all the most accessible spots, but if you've got space in your suitcase, it's definitely worthwhile bringing your own and checking out some of the less-visited parts of the coasts. Anywhere there's a reef (apart from those with dangerously large waves), you won't go wrong slipping into the water to see what's swimming around.

☑ Top Tips

▶ Ask to see dive operators' certificates or certification cards – no reputable shop will be offended by this request. To guide certified divers on a reef dive, guides must hold at least 'rescue diver' or preferably 'dive master' qualifications.

▶ At a minimum, a dive boat should carry oxygen and a first-aid kit. A radio or mobile phone is also important.

Green sea turtle

Best Diving

Gili Trawangan Dive shops and spots abound on Gili T. Free-diving is popular here, and there are reefs in all directions. (p126)

Nusa Lembongan There are dozens of great sites here and at the two neighbouring islands. (p90)

World Diving Excellent Nusa Lembongan operator leads trips and offers certification. It also organises trips to the deep and challenging waters off nearby Nusa Penida. (p90)

Crystal Divers Sanur's top dive shop gives great lessons and organises trips. (p86)

Best Snorkelling

Gili Trawangan Wander into water teeming with fish and reefs right off the beach. (p126)

Nusa Lembongan Reefs and mangroves combine for many fine sites. (p90)

Padangbai Nearby beach coves have fun snorkelling right off the beach. (p121)

Surya Water Sports Sanur's best water-sports shop offers boat trips for snorkellers. (p86)

Worth a Trip

Pulau Menjangan is Bali's best-known dive area and has a dozen superb dive sites. The diving is excellent – iconic tropical fish, soft corals, great visibility (usually), caves and a spectacular drop-off. It's located on the northwest coast of the island, and is best visited as part of an overnight jaunt to Pemuteran, which has resorts.

Best
Eating

Fusion cooking is the hallmark of inventive menus found across south Bali and Ubud. Creative chefs take techniques and influences from across the globe and combine them into menus that surprise and delight. On a list of reasons to visit Bali, the food – from humble Balinese to extravagantly global – must always be included.

LUCA TROVATO/GETTY IMAGES ©

Balinese Food

Balinese food is pungent and lively. The biting note of fresh ginger is matched by the heat of raw chillies, shrimp paste, palm sugar and tamarind. There is nothing shy about this cuisine.

You can taste South Indian, Malaysian and Chinese flavours in Balinese food. It has evolved from years of cross-cultural cook-ups and trading with sea-faring pioneers, and perhaps even pirates, across the seas of Asia.

Don't miss lunch at a warung, where you choose from an array of dishes that can be mixed and matched to your stomach's content. Spicy, vegetarian, nuanced, meaty, seafood – it's all here along with a choice of several kinds of rice.

Casual Fare

For a cuisine that is so nuanced, it may surprise that more often than not it is simply wolfed down. The Western idea of coming together doesn't apply to the Balinese, who eat when they are hungry. Gatherings involving food are saved for ceremonies and festivals. Rather, Balinese meals are most often cooked by vendors, whether stirring a roaring wok, pushing a cart (the ultimate convenience food) or slaving away all morning so that hordes can descend at lunch and lay waste to dozens of warung dishes.

☑ Top Tips

▶ Plunge into any Balinese food market and buy any fruit that looks unfamiliar. It costs little and (usually) tastes amazing.

▶ Much of the heat in Balinese food comes from the sambal. Ask for extra (not the commercial bottled stuff, the handmade kind) and earn respect – and enjoyment.

Balinese food

Best Top End

Sardine Beautiful food in a beautiful setting. (p56)

Locavore Ubud's most talked-about restaurant is a farm-to-table gem. (p113)

Mozaic Creativity mixed with lavish fare from an ambitious kitchen. (p113)

Best Local

Merah Putih Indonesia's cuisine is served with style (p55)

Warung Sulawesi Defines tasty Balinese warung fare. (p53)

Warung Pulau Kelapa Dishes from across Indonesia served with colour and flair. (p109)

Warung Eny Family-run gem, where if you like your meal, you can learn how to make it. (p53)

Gianyar's Night Market Browse this nightly carnival of the best local eats (p124)

Best Casual

Biku One of the island's most popular restaurants never hits a wrong note. (p39)

Three Monkeys Long-running pan-Asian fave

in Ubud on a rice field. (p112)

Lei Lei Seaside Barbeque The best of myriad choices for Jimbaran seafood. (p64)

Warung Soba The definitive New Agey Ubud restaurant is healthy and tasty. (p103)

Pica Surprisingly creative South American designed for sharing. (p111)

Om Burger Burgers served in a stylish surfer setting. (p75)

Alchemy Raw food with complex flavours, perfect after a stint of Ubud yoga. (p112)

Best
Surfing

Listen to the surfer tongues: Australian, American, Italian, Dutch, Japanese, Balinese (yes, lots of Balinese!) and many more are heard. People from all over the world come to Bali to surf, which shouldn't surprise anyone. Bali's surf breaks are legend and they are many. The series off Ulu Watu are among the world's best.

ANDREY ARTYKOV/GETTY IMAGES ©

Where to Surf

Swells come from the Indian Ocean, so the surf is on the southern side of the island and, strangely, on the northwest coast of Nusa Lembongan, where the swell funnels into the strait between there and the Bali coast.

In the dry season (around April to September), the west coast, from Ulu Watu to Echo Beach and beyond, has the best breaks; this is also when Nusa Lembongan works best. In the wet season surf the eastern side of the island.

South Bali has myriad surf schools and when it comes time to don the look, there are entire retail empires owned by people who were once just surfers, dude.

Best Surf Breaks

Kuta Beach Bali's original surf beach is still a winner. (p26)

Double Six Beach Great mix of tourists and locals. (p26)

Echo Beach Wild waves and plenty of spectators. (p51)

Ulu Watu Bali's best surf breaks are truly incredible. (p72)

Balangan Right off a great beach with fun cafes. (p72)

Bingin Close to cheap surfer lodgings, this isolated beach is worth the climb down a cliff. (p73)

Pantai Keramas East Coast beach and surf break that's attracting more and more top surfers. (p123)

Nusa Lembongan Three famous breaks are right off Jungutbatu Beach. (p90)

Best Surf Schools

Pro Surf School Long-running school that can get almost anyone surfing. (p27)

Rip Curl School of Surf Part of an entire surfing lifestyle empire. (p28)

Best
For Kids

Bali is a good place for kids. There's lots of kid-friendly fun to be had and the locals are especially enamoured of pint-sized visitors. Cool things to do include beaches, pools – almost every hotel has one, mysterious temples, monkeys, tourist parks geared to kids, ocean adventures, such as snorkelling, and a lot more.

FRANCO BANFI/GETTY IMAGES ©

The Balinese & Children

To the Balinese, children are considered part of the community and everyone, not just the parents, has a responsibility towards them. Little ones are a social asset when you travel and people will display great interest in any Western child they meet. Key kid details in Bahasa Indonesia: *bulau* (month), *tahun* (year), *laki-laki* (boy) and *perempuan* (girl).

Best Watery Fun

Rip Curl School of Surf Popular surf school has kids' programs. (p28)

Benoa Marine Recreation Oodles of aquatic fun. (p80)

Sanur Beach Mellow waters and lots of clean sand. (p86)

Surya Water Sports Tons of cool reasons to get wet. (p86)

Mushroom Bay Sheltered beach on Nusa Lembongan with water sports. (p91)

Best Amusement Parks

Canggu Club Has a new slide-filled water park. (p52)

Waterbom Park A wet, wild and watery kingdom. (p26)

Best Random Fun

Sacred Monkey Forest Sanctuary Indiana Jones–like temples in a forest filled with monkeys. (p106)

☑ Top Tips

▶ Look for beach vendors selling kites; huge breezy fun.

▶ An hour north of Ubud, **Elephant Safari Park** (☎0361-721480; www.bali adventuretours.com; Taro; tour incl transport adult/child US$65/44; ⊙8am-6pm) is home to retired logging elephants from other parts of Indonesia.

Pura Luhur Ulu Watu An ancient temple with sea views and, yes, monkeys. (p71)

JJ Bali Button Millions of cool buttons. (p57)

Bali Kite Festival Ginormous kites roaring overhead. (p89)

Best
Shopping

Bali's shops could occupy days of your holiday. Designer boutiques (Bali has a thriving fashion industry), slick galleries, wholesale emporiums and family-run workshops are just some of the choices. The shopping scene is like a form of primordial soup. New boutiques appear, old ones vanish, some change into something else while others move up the food chain.

MATT MUNRO/GETTY IMAGES ©

Bargaining

Price tags only make sporadic appearances in Bali's stores. Most everyday purchases require bargaining. A certain price flexibility even applies at many of Seminyak's trendiest boutiques (the only certain exceptions are international chains).

Although visitors used to forking out the total shown on the scanner may be intimidated by the need to negotiate, bargaining can be an enjoyable part of shopping in Bali. Maintain your sense of humour and remember the old bromide: 'Why pay retail?'. Try following these steps:

▶ Have some idea of what the item is worth.

▶ Establish a starting price – ask the seller for their price rather than making an initial offer.

▶ Your first price can be from one-third to two-thirds of the asking price – assuming that the asking price is not outrageous.

▶ With offers and counter-offers, move closer to an acceptable price.

▶ If you don't get to an acceptable price, you're entitled to walk – the vendor may call you back with a lower price.

▶ Note that when you name a price, you're committed – you must buy if your offer is accepted.

▶ Don't push if the prices really are set.

☑ **Top Tips**

▶ Much of Kuta, Legian and certain euphemistically named 'art markets' in Ubud, Seminyak and elsewhere are filled with junk that's not even made on Bali.

▶ The top-selling souvenir is the penis-shaped bottle-opener; the irony is that the imagery actually has deep roots in Balinese beliefs (penises abound in old temple carvings).

Pasar Badung, Denpasar

Best Clothes

Namu Nifty duds that are typical of Seminyak's fashion creativity. (p44)

Divine Diva Ultra-comfy womenswear you wished you'd packed. (p44)

Biasa One of Bali's classic fashion labels; it has an international reputation for its brilliant use of fabrics and materials. (p44)

Bamboo Blonde The cure for terminal frump. (p44)

Drifter High-end surfwear. (p43)

Goddess on the Go! Cottony cool clothes for women who want comfort and style on the road; the name sums it up. (p117)

Surfer Girl Another of Bali's iconic surf brands. (p33)

Best for Browsing

JJ Bali Button Fun for the whole family; buttons pack easy too. (p57)

Hobo Clever housewares designed and made on Bali. (p57)

Ganesha Bookshop Bali's best bookshop has carefully chosen selections. (p116)

Bathe Fun stuff for the house that smells good. (p42)

Pasar Badung Bali's large central market has it all. (p96)

Best Textiles

Adil Standout dealer of beautiful local fabrics. (p96)

Threads of Life Indonesian Textile Arts Center Handmade traditional Bali fabrics. (p116)

Best
LGBT Bali

Bali easily ranks as one of the world's most tolerant LGBT travel destinations. Much of this stems from the beliefs and attitudes ingrained in the Balinese. People are accepted as they are, judging others is considered extremely rude and there's a limited macho culture where masculinity is easily threatened. Anywhere listed in this book can be considered gay-friendly.

AGUNG PARAMESWARA / STRINGER/GETTY IMAGES ©

The Scene

Homosexuality among visitors has a long tradition on Bali. Many of the island's most influential expatriate artists have been more-or-less openly gay.

Many Balinese openly become involved with visitors of the same sex, although this is far more common with men than with women. There is no thought given to possible social ramifications among their friends, family or neighbours. In fact Bali is something of a haven for gays from across Indonesia.

One of the converse effects about having gay life so much a part of life on Bali is that there are relatively few 'gay' places, although many bars and clubs of Seminyak's Jl Abimanyu form a nexus of gay Bali.

Best LGBT Nightlife

Bali Jo Fab drag shows draw a mixed crowd; several other clubs are nearby. (p39)

Dix Club Wild and woolly fun through the night. (p39)

☑ Top Tips

▶ Homosexual behaviour is not illegal on Bali.

▶ Gay men in Indonesia are referred to as *homo,* or *gay,* and are quite distinct from female impersonators called *waria.*

▶ In general Bali is one of the most gay-friendly destinations in Southeast Asia.

Best
Festivals &
Ceremonies

A crash of the gamelan and traffic screeches to a halt as a mob of elegantly dressed people comes flying by bearing pyramids of fruit, tasselled parasols and a furred, masked Barong (lion-like character) or two: it's a temple procession disappearing as suddenly as it appeared, with no more than the fleeting sparkle of gold and white silk and hibiscus petals in its wake. Dozens occur daily across Bali.

JOHN W BANAGAN/GETTY IMAGES ©

Temple Festivals

Each of the thousands of temples on the island has a 'temple birthday' known as an *odalan*. These are celebrated once every Balinese year of 210 days or every 354 to 356 days on the *caka* calendar (yes it's bewildering; there are priests who do nothing but try to sort out the calendar).

Best Special Days

Nyepi The year's most special day is marked by total inactivity – to convince evil spirits that Bali is uninhabited, so they'll leave the island alone. The night before, huge papier-mâché monsters (*ogoh-ogoh*) go up in flames. You'll see these built by enthusiastic locals in communities island-wide in the weeks before. Held in March or early April.

Galungan One of Bali's major festivals. During a 10-day period, all the gods come down to earth for the festivities, which celebrate the death of a legendary tyrant called Mayadenawa. Barong prance from temple to temple and village to village (many of these processions consist entirely of children), and locals rejoice with feasts and visits to families.

Kuningan At the culmination of Galungan, the Balinese say thanks and goodbye to the gods. You'll see large temple ceremonies across the island – and likely be caught in long traffic queues as a result. Abandon your vehicle and join the scene. On beaches, families dressed spotlessly in white look for purification from the ocean's waters.

☑ **Top Tip**

▶ Ask any locals you meet what *odalan* (temple festivals) are happening. Seeing one will be a highlight of your trip, particularly if it is at a major temple. Foreigners are welcome to watch the festivities, but be unobtrusive and dress modestly.

Best
Art

Until visitors arrived in great numbers, the acts of painting and carving were purely to decorate temples and shrines as well as to enrich ceremonies. Today, with galleries and craft shops everywhere, paintings are stacked up on gallery floors and you may trip over carvings in both stone and wood. Amid the tat, however, you will find a great deal of beautiful work.

TOM COCKREM/GETTY IMAGES ©

Painting

Balinese painting is the art form most influenced by Western ideas. Ubud's art museums and galleries have a range of beautiful paintings. Styles range from abstract works of incredible colour to beautiful and evocative representations – some highly idealised – of island life.

Crafts

Bali is a showroom of Indonesia's creativity, including fabrics and crafts from across the archipelago.

Carving was traditionally done for temples and the Balinese are experts, with works – such as a frog using a leaf as an umbrella – often showing their sense of humour.

Masks are a popular purchase. The mask maker must know the movements that each performer uses; the results are both dramatic and colourful.

Best Museums & Galleries

Museum Le Mayeur House and gallery of one of Bali's most influential painters. (p85)

Agung Rai Museum of Art Excellent private museum in Ubud. (p106)

Museum Puri Lukisan A great history of Balinese art. (p106)

Pasifika Museum Large museum with fine works from Bali and the region. (p79)

Neka Art Museum Has paintings by many of the local greats. (p106)

☑ Top Tips

▶ Bali's arts and crafts originated in honouring fertility of the land and Dewi Sri, the rice goddess.

▶ Batubulan, on the main road from south Bali to Ubud, is a major stone-carving centre. Figures line both sides of the road, and carvers can be seen in action in the many workshops.

Museum Negeri Propinsi Bali The island's main museum has art from the ages. (p95)

Kendra Gallery Small gallery with top-notch shows in Seminyak. (p43)

Survival Guide

Survival Guide

Before You Go

When to Go

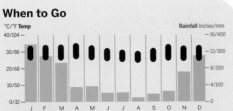

°C/°F Temp
Rainfall Inches/mm

→ High Season (Jul & Aug) Rates zip up by 50% or more; many hotels are booked far ahead. Christmas and New Year are equally expensive and crowded.

→ Shoulder (May, Jun & Sep) Coincides with the best weather (drier, less humid); some deals but last-minute bookings possible; best time for diving, since the water is clear.

→ Low Season (Jan–Apr, Oct & Nov) Deals everywhere; rainy season, however, rainfall is rarely excessive.

Book Your Stay

→ It's common for people to move around Bali even for short stays. Splitting your time between several locations is typical.

→ Ubud is best enjoyed overnight, once day-trippers are gone and dance performances are on.

→ With a budget of US$100 a night you can find nice midrange hotels virtually everywhere (often for less).

→ Villas can be surprisingly affordable: under US$200 for your own compound.

→ Beware chain hotels offering deals that are located far from the beaches and nightlife.

Useful Websites

→ Bali Discovery (www.balidiscovery.com) A Bali-based tour company with locally sourced deals on hotels and villas.

→ Booking.com (www.booking.com) Booking site that covers almost every place to stay in Bali.

→ Agoda (www.agoda.com) Another major site, along with Booking.com.

→ Lonely Planet (www.lonelyplanet.com/indonesia/bali) Destination information, hotel bookings, traveller forum and more.

Best Budget

Ned's Hide-Away (nedshide@dps.centrin.net.id) The Ned's family are real charmers. There are 16 good-value basic rooms behind the Bintang Supermarket in Seminyak. A newish expansion includes both extra-cheap and more plush rooms.

Widi Homestay (widihomestay@yahoo.co.id) There's no faux hipster vibe here with fake nihilist bromides, just a spotless, friendly family-run homestay. The four rooms have hot water and air-con; Canggu beach is barely 100m away.

Adi's Home Stay The nine bungalow style rooms facing a garden are new and comfy, and it's down a very small lane near the beach parking in Bingin. It has a small cafe.

Ni Nyoman Warini Bungalows There's a whole pod of simple family compounds with rooms for rent on a little footpath off Jl Hanomani in Ubud. It's quiet, and without even trying you'll find yourself enjoying the rhythms of family life. The eight rooms here have hot water and traditional bamboo furniture.

Best Midrange

Temple Lodge (www. thetemplelodge.com) Artsy and beautiful just begin to describe this collection of huts and cottages made from thatch, driftwood and other natural materials in Bingin. It sits on a jutting shelf on the cliffs above the surf breaks and there are superb views from the infinity pool and some of the seven units. You can arrange for meals and there are morning yoga classes.

Oka Wati Hotel (www. okawatihotel.com) Owner Oka Wati is a lovely lady who grew up in Ubud. The 19 rooms here have large verandahs where the delightful staff will deliver your choice of breakfast (do not

miss the house-made yoghurt). The decor features vintage details like four-poster beds; some rooms view a small rice field and river valley. Follow narrow footpaths to get here.

Matahari Cottages (www. matahariubud.com) This delightful place in Ubud has 15 flamboyant, themed rooms, including the 'Batavia Princess' and the 'Indian Pasha'. The library is a vision out of a 1920s fantasy. It also boasts a self-proclaimed 'jungle Jacuzzi', an upscale way to replicate the old Bali tradition of river-bathing. There's a multicourse breakfast and high tea.

Mutiara Bali (www.mutiara bali.com) Although hidden on a small road behind Jl Kayu Aya in Seminyak, the Mutiara is close to fine dining (200m) and the beach (800m). There are 29 good-sized and nicely furnished rooms in two-storey blocks around a frangipani-draped pool area, plus 17 private villas.

Alam Indah (www.alamindah bali.com) Just south of the Monkey Forest in Nyuhkuning in Ubud, this isolated and spacious resort has 16 rooms that

are beautifully finished in natural materials to traditional designs. The Wos Valley views are entrancing, especially from the multilevel pool area. A companion property, Alam Jiwa, is a 10-minute walk further into the rice fields. Great cafe!

Best Top End

Oberoi (www.oberoihotels. com) The beautifully understated Oberoi has been a refined Balinese-style beachside retreat in Seminyak since 1971. All accommodation options have private verandahs, and as you move up the food chain, additional features include walled villas, ocean views and private pools. With a cafe overlooking the almost-private sweep of beach to the numerous luxuries, this is a place to spoil yourself.

Buah Bali Villas (www. thebuahbali.com) This small development in Kerobokan has only seven villas, which range in size from one to two bedrooms. Like the many other nearby villa hotels, each unit has a private pool in a walled compound and a nice open-air living area. The location is superb: hotspots such as

Biku and Potato Head are a five-minute walk away.

Hotel Tugu Bali (www.tugu hotels.com) Right at Batu Bolong Beach, Canggu, this exclusive hotel blurs the boundaries between museum and gallery, especially the Walter Spies and Le Mayeur Pavilions, where memorabilia from the artists' decorates the rooms. There's a spa and customised dining options.

Warwick Ibah Luxury Villas & Spa (www.warwick ibah.com) Overlooking the rushing waters and rice-clad hills of the Wos Valley, Ubud, the Ibah offers re-fined luxury in 15 spacious, stylish individual suites and villas that combine ancient and modern details. Each could be a feature in an interior design magazine. The swimming pool is set into the hillside amid gardens and lavish stone carvings.

Amandari (www.amanresorts. com) In Kedewatan village, Ubud, the storied Amandari does everything with the charm and grace of a classical Balinese dancer. Superb views over the jungle and down to the river – the 30m green-tiled swimming pool seems to drop right over the edge – are just some of the inducements. The 30 private pavilions may prove inescapable.

Uma by Como (www.como hotels.com) One of Ubud's most attractive properties has 46 rooms in a variety of sizes, but all have a relaxed naturalistic style that goes well with the gorgeous views over the gardens and the river valley beyond. Service and amenities such as the restaurant are superb.

Arriving in Bali

Ngurah Rai Airport

➡ Prepaid taxis from Bali's airport are the most common way to get to your accommodation.

➡ Most hotels will pick you up at the airport for a fee, from US$10 to US$50 (typical for the fairly long haul to Ubud). This can be especially nice if you are arriving after a long flight and/or it's your first visit to Bali. A hotel rep will be waiting in the arrivals area with your name written on a sign-board.

➡ Unless you absolutely, positively need help with your bags, refuse the service of the arrivals area porters as fees can be surprising (if needed, negotiate a price in advance).

➡ When you're departing, have 200,000Rp in exact change for departure tax.

Getting Around

Boat

☑ **Best for...** Reaching Nusa Lembongan and Gili Trawangan.

➡ Fast boats link Bali to nearby islands.

➡ Advertised travel times can be false; double the time quoted.

➡ Fares may seem pricey but are negotiable; some services include hotel pickups on Bali.

➡ Boats are unregulated and there have been accidents. Go with established companies and confirm there are life boats and easily accessed life pre-servers before departure.

Car

☑ **Best for...** Exploring completely on your own.

➡ Car rentals cost US$25 to US$50 per day. Offers are everywhere. However, you'll have to deal with Bali's horrible traffic and myriad ways to get lost.

Car & Driver
☑ **Best for...** Maximum flexibility, minimal fuss.

➡ For a fee of US$40 to US$60 per day you can arrange for a driver and vehicle to take you virtually anywhere you want on Bali, stopping off wherever you want. It's easiest to arrange this through your accommodation.

➡ Most drivers are charming people who will add delight to your journey; however, if your driver pressures you to stop for food at a tourist restaurant surrounded by tour buses or any kind of souvenir shop, refuse. They are probably getting a kickback; use a different driver next time.

Motorbike
☑ **Best for...** Saving money, beating traffic.

➡ Offers for motorbike rental are everywhere. Daily costs are US$5 to US$20. Accidents are common; helmets are required. Some bikes come equipped with surfboard racks.

Taxi
☑ **Best for...** Most trips.

➡ Bali taxis are plentiful and surprisingly cheap. They are the preferred means of travel for most trips around south Bali.

➡ Always insist on the meter and get out of any cab that refuses.

➡ The most reliable company remains **Bluebird Taxi** (☎ 0361-701111; www.bluebirdgroup.com); you can call for pick-up or use their app. Look for the 'Bluebird Group' sticker over the windshield (many other taxis try to ape the look).

Tourist Bus
☑ **Best for...** Saving money.

➡ **Perama** (www.peramatour.com) runs air-con buses (average fare 100,000Rp) for tourists between Kuta, Sanur, Ubud and points east. However, the buses don't come close to Seminyak, Kerobokan or anyplace on the Bukit Peninsula, such as Ulu Watu or Nusa Dua. Also, the stops are sometimes inconvenient.

Essential Information

Business Hours
Standard hours are as follows; significant variations are shown in the listings.
Restaurants and cafes 8am to 10pm daily
Shops and services catering to visitors 9am to 8pm daily

Electricity

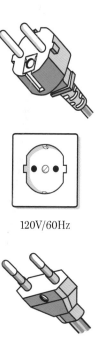

120V/60Hz

220V/230V/50Hz

Emergency
➡ If you have a problem that needs police or

medical attention, ask the nearest hotel or restaurant as there are no useful central numbers for visitors to call.

Health

☑ **Top Tip** Don't drink tap water; opt for cheaply available bottled water (and reuse bottles when possible). Ice in tourist places is normally made with filtered water at a central plant – if it is uniform in shape, it should be safe.

➡ There are several clinics and hospitals in south Bali with Western standards. The most popular, and expensive, is **BIMC** (📞0361-761263; www.bimc bali.com; JI Ngurah Rai 100X; 🕐24hr). Hotels can make recommendations.

➡ Ensure that you have travel insurance that covers medical evacuation.

➡ Rabies is a major problem on Bali; if you are bitten or come into contact with a stray animal seek medical attention immediately as rabies is fatal.

➡ Dengue fever is a problem; wear mosquito repellents that contain DEET.

➡ Travellers diarrhoea is common. Stay hydrated and if it doesn't improve in 24 hours, consider antibiotics from a pharmacy.

➡ *Arak*, an alcoholic beverage made from palm, is usually legitimate and is a popular drink. However there have been poisonings and deaths due to adulterated *arak*. The safest approach is to avoid it; never accept any outside of established and reputable cafes and restaurants.

Money

☑ **Top Tip** You can use ATMs for money during your trip. Bring US$100 in case the network goes down or there is a problem with your card and you need backup.

➡ Indonesia's unit of currency is the rupiah (Rp). There are coins worth 50Rp, 100Rp, 500Rp and 1000Rp. Notes come in denominations of 1000Rp, 2000Rp, 5000Rp, 10,000Rp, 20,000Rp, 50,000Rp and 100,000Rp.

➡ US dollars are the most convertible currency.

➡ Always carry a good supply of rupiah in small denominations. Individuals will struggle to make change for a 50,000Rp note or larger.

ATMs

➡ There are ATMs all over Bali (with the notable exception of Nusa Lembongan); Circle K convenience stores are reliable locations.

➡ Exchange rates for ATM withdrawals are usually OK, but see if your home bank will hit you with outrageous fees.

Credit Cards

➡ Visa, MasterCard and Amex are accepted by most larger businesses.

Moneychangers

➡ Exchange rates offered by moneychangers with signs along the road may seem better than banks, but that's because the difference is often made up through scams.

➡ Central Kuta Money Exchange is a reliable chain of money exchanges found across south Bali and Ubud.

Tipping

➡ Tipping a set percentage is not expected in Bali, but if the service is good, it's appropriate to leave 5000Rp or 10% or more.

➡ Most midrange hotels and restaurants and all top-end hotels and restaurants add 21% to the bill for tax and service (known as 'plus plus'). This service component is distributed among hotel staff (one hopes).

➡ Hand cash directly to individuals if you think they

deserve recognition for their service.

➡ Tip good taxi drivers, guides, people giving you a massage or fetching you a beer on the beach etc; 5000Rp to 10,000Rp is generous.

Public Holidays

☑ **Top Tip** Check if Nyepi falls during your trip as Bali shuts down for 24 hours.

The following holidays are celebrated throughout Indonesia. Many of the dates change according to the phase of the moon (not by month) or by religious calendar, so the following are estimates only.

➡ **Tahun Baru Masehi** New Year's Day) 1 January

➡ **Idul Adha** (Muslim festival of sacrifice) February

➡ **Muharram** (Islamic New Year) February/March

➡ **Nyepi** (Hindu New Year) March/April

➡ **Hari Paskah** (Good Friday) April

➡ **Ascension of Christ** April/May

➡ **Hari Waisak** (Buddha's birth, enlightenment and death) April/May

➡ **Maulud Nabi Mohammed/Hari Natal** (Prophet Mohammed's birthday) Date varies

➡ **Idul Fitri** (End of Ramadan) July

➡ **Hari Proklamasi Kemerdekaan** (Indonesian Independence Day) 17 August

➡ **Isra Miraj Nabi Mohammed** (Ascension of the Prophet Mohammed) September

➡ **Hari Natal** (Christmas Day) 25 December

Safe Travel

☑ **Top Tip** Bali is fairly safe, so relax and enjoy.

➡ Violent crime is uncommon, but bag-snatching, pickpocketing and theft from rooms and parked cars is on the increase. Don't take drugs to Bali nor buy any while there. Penalties are severe.

➡ Avoid beaches and the ocean around streams running into the water after rain, because all sorts of unsavoury matter may be present.

➡ Be careful when walking on the sidewalk or pavement; gaping holes can cause severe injury. Carry a torch/flashlight at night.

Telephone

☑ **Top Tip** If a Bali phone number doesn't work, try adding a four between the area code and the number. Extra digits are being added to numbers to allow for more lines. Automated prompts announcing a number change don't always work.

➡ SIM cards on Bali cost only 5000Rp (anything more should include credit), coming with cheap rates for calling other countries, starting at US$0.20 per minute. You can buy them everywhere.

➡ Roaming rates without a local SIM card for your mobile can be outrageous.

➡ Most hotel wi-fi service in south Bali and Ubud will allow Skype to work.

Toilets

➡ Western-style toilets are almost universally common in tourist areas.

➡ During the day, look for a cafe or hotel and smile (public toilets only exist at some major sights).

Visas

☑ **Top Tip** Carry US$35 in exact change for the visa on arrival at Bali's airport.

➡ Citizens of over 60 countries, including all major ones, can purchase a visa on arrival at Bali's airport for US$35. It is good for 30 days. You can renew it once while on Bali.

Index

Behind the Scenes

Send Us Your Feedback

We love to hear from travellers – your comments help make our books better. We read every word, and we guarantee that your feedback goes straight to the authors. Visit **lonelyplanet.com/contact** to submit your updates and suggestions.

Note: We may edit, reproduce and incorporate your comments in Lonely Planet products such as guidebooks, websites and digital products, so let us know if you don't want your comments reproduced or your name acknowledged. For a copy of our privacy policy visit lonelyplanet.com/privacy.

Ryan's Thanks

For this, my 101st guidebook for Lonely Planet, many thanks to friends including Patticakes, Ibu Cat, Hanafi, Stuart, Suzanne, the indefatigable Ketut, Rucina, Nicoline, Eliot Cohen, Jamie James, Kerry and Milt Turner, Pascal & Pika and many more.

Acknowledgments

Cover photograph: Cleansing ceremony. Kuta Beach. Cintract Romain/Alamy.

This Book

This 4th edition of Lonely Planet's *Pocket Bali* guidebook was researched and written by Ryan Ver Berkmoes. The previous two editions were also researched and written by Ryan Ver Berkmoes.

This guidebook was produced by the following: **Destination Editor** Sarah Reid **Product Editor** Amanda Williamson **Senior Cartographer** Julie Sheridan **Book Designer** Jessica Rose **Assisting Editors** Nigel Chin, Victoria Harrison **Assisting Book**

Designer Wibowo Rusli **Cover Researcher** Naomi Parker **Thanks to** Jennifer Bray, Sarah Collins, Ryan Evans, Isabelle Huber, Elizabeth Jones, Sheldon Levis, Claire Naylor, Karyn Noble, Martine Power, Angela Tinson

Our Writer

Ryan Ver Berkmoes

Ryan Ver Berkmoes was first entranced by the echoing beat of a Balinese gamelan in 1993. On his visits since he has explored almost every corner of the island – along with Nusas Lembongan and Penida, the Gilis and Lombok. Just when he thinks Bali holds no more surprises, he finds, for example, a new seaside temple on nobody's map. Away from the gamelans, Ryan writes about travel and more at ryanverberkmoes.com and on Twitter (@ryanvb).

Published by Lonely Planet Publications Pty Ltd
ABN 36 005 607 983
4th edition – April 2015
ISBN 978 1 74220 8961
© Lonely Planet 2015 Photographs © as indicated 2015
10 9 8 7 6 5 4 3 2 1
Printed in China

Although the authors and Lonely Planet have taken all reasonable care in preparing this book, we make no warranty about the accuracy or completeness of its content and, to the maximum extent permitted, disclaim all liability arising from its use.